Foundation

Pearson Edexcel GCSE (9-1)

History

Early Elizabethan England, 1558–1588

Series Editor: Angela Leonard   Author: Georgina Blair

Pearson

Published by Pearson Education Limited, 80 Strand, London, WC2R 0RL.

www.pearsonschoolsandfecolleges.co.uk

Copies of official specifications for all Edexcel qualifications may be found on the website: www.edexcel.com

Text © Pearson Education Limited 2018

Series editor: Angela Leonard
Designed by Colin Tilley Loughrey, Pearson Education Limited
Typeset by Phoenix Photosetting, Chatham, Kent
Original illustrations © Pearson Education Limited
Illustrated by KJA Artists Illustration Agency, Phoenix Photosetting, Chatham, Kent and QBS Learning.

Cover design by Colin Tilley Loughrey
Picture research by Christine Martin
Cover photo © Bridgeman Art Library Ltd: National Portrait Gallery, London, UK

The right of Georgina Blair to be identified as author of this work has been asserted by her in accordance with the Copyright, Designs and Patents Act 1988.

First published 2018

24
10 9 8 7 6 5

British Library Cataloguing in Publication Data
A catalogue record for this book is available from the British Library.
ISBN 978 1 292 25832 4

A note from the publisher
1. While the publishers have made every attempt to ensure that advice on the qualification and its assessment is accurate, the official specification and associated assessment guidance materials are the only authoritative source of information and should always be referred to for definitive guidance.

Pearson examiners have not contributed to any sections in this resource relevant to examination papers for which they have responsibility.

2. Pearson has robust editorial processes, including answer and fact checks, to ensure the accuracy of the content in this publication, and every effort is made to ensure this publication is free of errors. We are, however, only human, and occasionally errors do occur. Pearson is not liable for any misunderstandings that arise as a result of errors in this publication, but it is our priority to ensure that the content is accurate. If you spot an error, please do contact us at resourcescorrections@pearson.com so we can make sure it is corrected.

Websites
Pearson Education Limited is not responsible for the content of any external internet sites. It is essential for tutors to preview each website before using it in class so as to ensure that the URL is still accurate, relevant and appropriate. We suggest that tutors bookmark useful websites and consider enabling students to access them through the school/college intranet.

Contents

How to use this book

What's covered?

This book covers the British Depth study on Early Elizabethan England, 1558-88. This unit makes up 20% of your GCSE course, and will be examined in Paper 2.

Depth studies cover a short period of time, and require you to know about society, people and events in detail. You need to understand how the different aspects of the period fit together and affect each other. This book also explains the different types of exam questions you will need to answer, and includes advice and example answers to help you improve.

Features

As well as a clear, detailed explanation of the key knowledge you will need, you will also find a number of features in the book:

Key terms

Where you see a word followed by an asterisk, like this: Reformation*, you will be able to find a Key Terms box on that page that explains what the word means.

> **Key term**
>
> **The Reformation***
>
> A challenge to the teachings and power of the Roman Catholic Church. This movement is said to have begun in Europe in 1517.

Activities

Every few pages, you'll find a box containing some activities designed to help check and embed knowledge and get you to really think about what you've studied. The activities start simple, but might get more challenging as you work through them.

Summaries and Checkpoints

At the end of each chunk of learning, the main points are summarised in a series of bullet points – great for embedding the core knowledge, and handy for revision.

Checkpoints help you to check and reflect on your learning. The Strengthen section helps you to consolidate knowledge and understanding, and check that you've grasped the basic ideas and skills. The Challenge questions push you to go beyond just understanding the information, and into evaluation and analysis of what you've studied.

Sources and Interpretations

Although source work and interpretations do not appear in Paper 2, you'll still find interesting contemporary material throughout the books, showing what people from the period said, thought or created, helping you to build your understanding of people in the past.

The book also includes extracts from the work of historians, showing how experts have interpreted the events you've been studying.

1.1 The situation on Elizabeth's accession

Source C

Elizabeth I (1558–1603) at her coronation, painted after 1600 by an unknown artist.

Challenges at home and from abroad
- profits of justice (fines, people convicted of cri
- loans (sometimes peo

Interpretation 1

Historians Turvey and Heard look at the effectiveness of Elizabeth's settlement in *Change and Protest 1536–88: Mid-Tudor Crises?* (1999).

… the Settlement had mixed success. It largely succeeded in establishing a broadly based national Church which excluded as few people as possible. … On the other hand, the Settlement not only failed to attract the Puritans but… devout [seriously committed] Catholics were likewise marginalised [sidelined] with the consequence of encouraging opposition and non-conformity.

Extend your knowledge

These features contain useful additional information that adds depth to your knowledge, and to your answers. The information is closely related to the key issues in the unit, and questions are sometimes included, helping you to link the new details to the main content.

> **Extend your knowledge**
>
> **Davy Ingram**
>
> One of the most famous accounts of the Americas was written by Davy Ingram. He survived a Spanish attack on Drake and Hawkins at San Juan de Ulúa in Mexico and walked 3,000 miles north up the Atlantic coast of America. He told fantastic tales of great wealth to be found, including precious metals (buckets made of silver, great lumps of gold), minerals, fertile soil and bright red sheep and rabbits. These tales encouraged more voyages of exploration.

Exam-style questions and tips

The book also includes extra exam-style questions you can use to practise. These appear in the chapters and are accompanied by a tip to help you get started on an answer.

Exam-style question, Section B

Explain why the Catholic threat to Elizabeth I increased after 1566.

You may use the following in your answer:

* The Dutch Revolt
* Mary, Queen of Scots' arrival in England in 1568.

You must also use information of your own. **12 marks**

Exam tip

Don't just describe events. You must focus on reasons for the Catholic threat against Elizabeth becoming more serious.

Recap pages

At the end of each chapter, you'll find a page designed to help you to consolidate and reflect on the chapter as a whole. Each recap page includes a recall quiz, ideal for quickly checking your knowledge or for revision. Recap pages also include activities designed to help you summarise and analyse what you've learned, and also reflect on how each chapter links to other parts of the unit.

THINKING HISTORICALLY

These activities are designed to help you develop a better understanding of how history is constructed, and are focused on the key areas of Evidence, Interpretations, Cause & Consequence and Change & Continuity. In the British Depth Study, you will come across activities on Cause & Consequence, as this is a key focus for this unit.

The Thinking Historically approach has been developed in conjunction with Dr Arthur Chapman and the Institute of Education, UCL. It is based on research into the misconceptions that can hold students back in history.

 Cause and Consequence (3c&d) —— conceptual map reference

The Thinking Historically conceptual map can be found at: www.pearsonschools.co.uk/thinkinghistoricallygcse

WRITING HISTORICALLY

At the end of most chapters is a spread dedicated to helping you improve your writing skills. These include simple techniques you can use in your writing to make your answers clearer, more precise and better focused on the question you're answering.

The Writing Historically approach is based on the *Grammar for Writing* pedagogy developed by a team at the University of Exeter and popular in many English departments. Each spread uses examples from the preceding chapter, so it's relevant to what you've just been studying.

Preparing for your exams

At the back of the book, you'll find a special section dedicated to explaining and exemplifying the new Edexcel GCSE History exams. Advice on the demands of this paper, written by Angela Leonard, helps you prepare for and approach the exam with confidence. Each question type is explained through annotated sample answers at two levels, showing clearly how answers can be improved.

Pearson Progression Scale: This icon indicates the Step that a sample answer has been graded at on the Pearson Progression Scale.

This book is also available as an online ActiveBook, which can be licensed for your whole institution.

Timeline: Elizabethan England

Events at home

1558
Elizabeth I is crowned Queen of England after the death of her sister, Mary I

1563
Statute of Artificers

1559
Elizabeth implements her religious settlement, including the Act of Supremacy, Act of Uniformity and the Royal Injunctions

1568
Mary, Queen of Scots, flees to England from Scotland

1569
The Revolt of the Northern Earls to place Mary, Queen of Scots, on the throne

1570
Pope Pius V excommunicates Elizabeth from the Catholic Church

1571
The Ridolfi plot

1572
Vagabonds Act

1576
Poor Relief Act

1555	1560	1565	1570	1575

1559
Treaty of Cateau-Cambrésis

1560
Treaty of Edinburgh

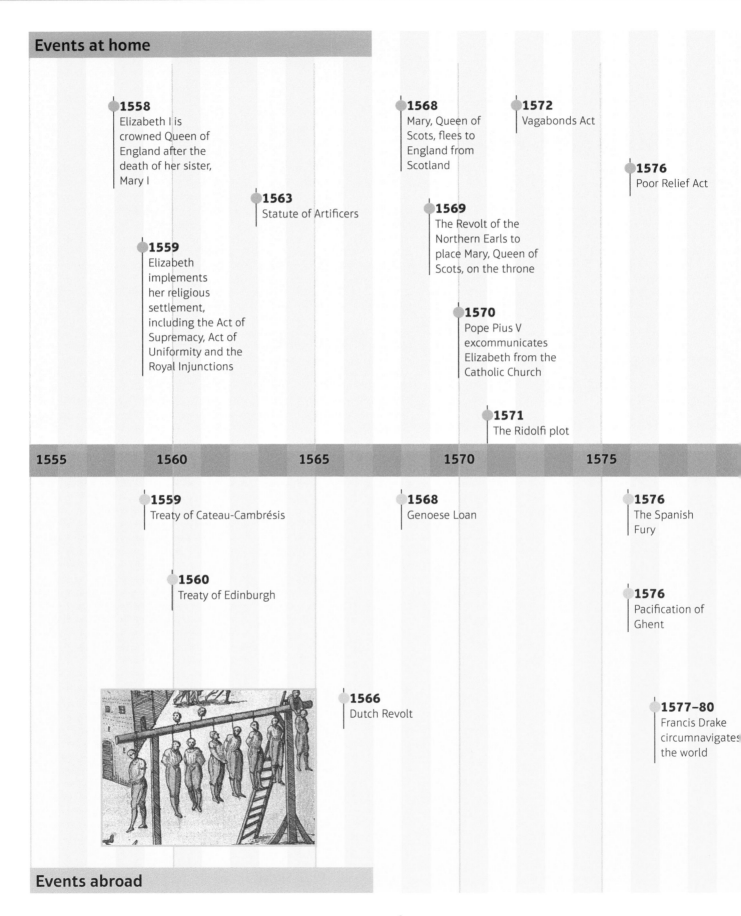

1566
Dutch Revolt

1568
Genoese Loan

1576
The Spanish Fury

1576
Pacification of Ghent

1577–80
Francis Drake circumnavigates the world

Events abroad

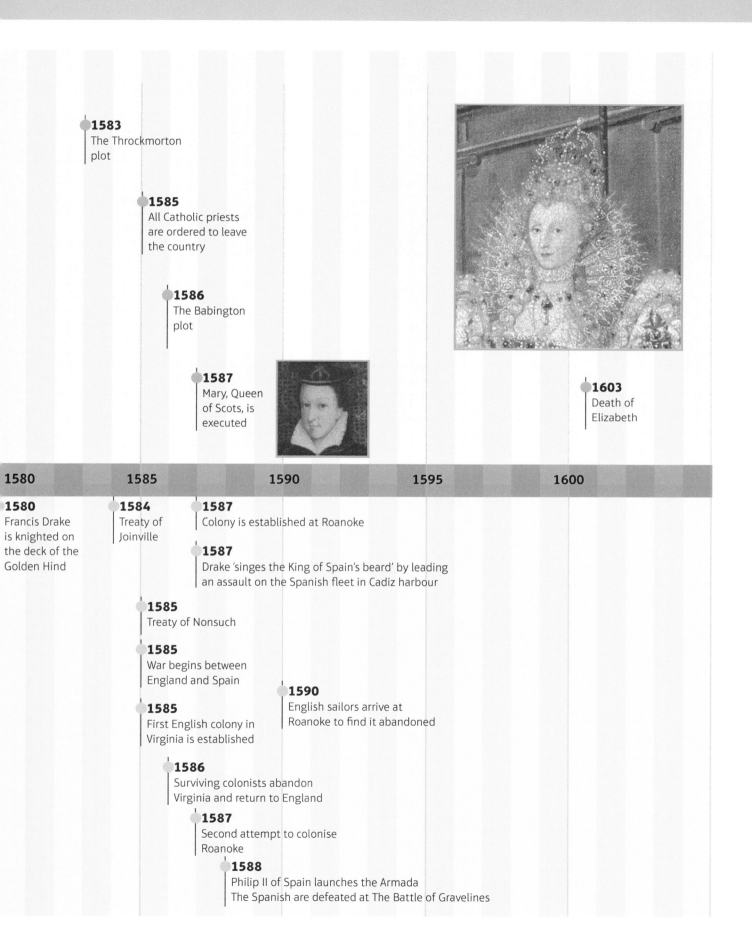

1583
The Throckmorton plot

1585
All Catholic priests are ordered to leave the country

1586
The Babington plot

1587
Mary, Queen of Scots, is executed

1603
Death of Elizabeth

1580   1585   1590   1595   1600

1580
Francis Drake is knighted on the deck of the Golden Hind

1584
Treaty of Joinville

1587
Colony is established at Roanoke

1587
Drake 'singes the King of Spain's beard' by leading an assault on the Spanish fleet in Cadiz harbour

1585
Treaty of Nonsuch

1585
War begins between England and Spain

1585
First English colony in Virginia is established

1590
English sailors arrive at Roanoke to find it abandoned

1586
Surviving colonists abandon Virginia and return to England

1587
Second attempt to colonise Roanoke

1588
Philip II of Spain launches the Armada
The Spanish are defeated at The Battle of Gravelines

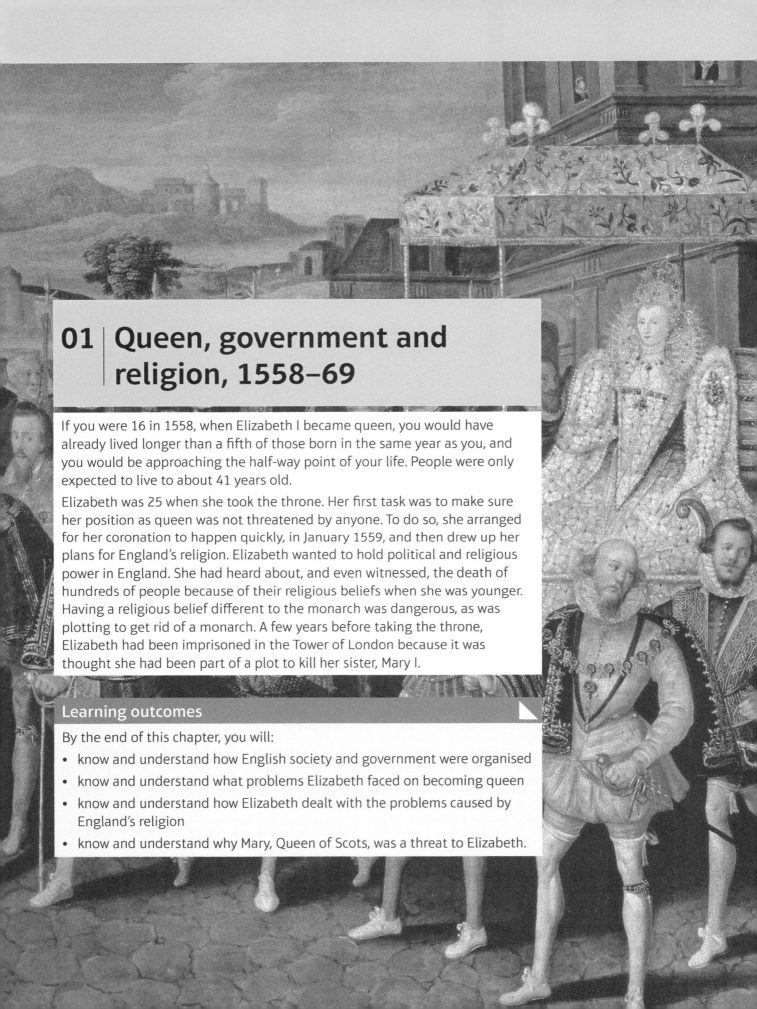

01 | Queen, government and religion, 1558–69

If you were 16 in 1558, when Elizabeth I became queen, you would have already lived longer than a fifth of those born in the same year as you, and you would be approaching the half-way point of your life. People were only expected to live to about 41 years old.

Elizabeth was 25 when she took the throne. Her first task was to make sure her position as queen was not threatened by anyone. To do so, she arranged for her coronation to happen quickly, in January 1559, and then drew up her plans for England's religion. Elizabeth wanted to hold political and religious power in England. She had heard about, and even witnessed, the death of hundreds of people because of their religious beliefs when she was younger. Having a religious belief different to the monarch was dangerous, as was plotting to get rid of a monarch. A few years before taking the throne, Elizabeth had been imprisoned in the Tower of London because it was thought she had been part of a plot to kill her sister, Mary I.

Learning outcomes

By the end of this chapter, you will:

- know and understand how English society and government were organised
- know and understand what problems Elizabeth faced on becoming queen
- know and understand how Elizabeth dealt with the problems caused by England's religion
- know and understand why Mary, Queen of Scots, was a threat to Elizabeth.

1.1 The situation on Elizabeth's accession

Learning outcomes

- Understand the structure of Elizabethan society in 1558.
- Understand the circumstances Elizabeth I found herself in when she came to the throne, including doubts about her right to be queen.
- Understand the challenges Elizabeth faced, both at home and abroad, during the early years of her reign.

Society and government in 1558

Elizabethan England was often a violent and dangerous place. As there was no police force or permanent army, keeping order relied upon everyone knowing their place in society. Equality* in society was not important to Elizabethans.

Society

Where you fitted in Elizabethan society was usually decided by how much land you had and whether you owned or rented it. About 90% of England's population lived and worked in the countryside. Figure 1.1 shows the different hierarchies in Elizabethan towns and the countryside.

At the top of this hierarchy* was the king or queen. In the countryside, next came the nobility and gentry who owned lots of land. Then came yeomen who owned smaller amounts of land, followed by tenant farmers who rented land to farm. Below this were the farm labourers who did not have their own land but worked for those above them. At the bottom of the hierarchy were people who had no jobs or homes.

In towns, the hierarchy was based on wealth and occupation. Wealthy **merchants*** were at the top, followed by **professionals***, such as lawyers and doctors. Next came skilled craftsmen, such as carpenters or tailors. They organised themselves into guilds*, and employed apprentices*. **Unskilled labourers** and the unemployed came at the bottom of society.

Key terms

Equality*

Treating everyone the same.

Hierarchy*

The order of people in a society.

Merchants*

People who buy and sell goods.

Professionals*

People who have trained to do a particular job.

Guilds*

A group of craftsmen or tradesmen who check that their craft or trade follows certain rules.

Apprentices*

People learning a trade or skill.

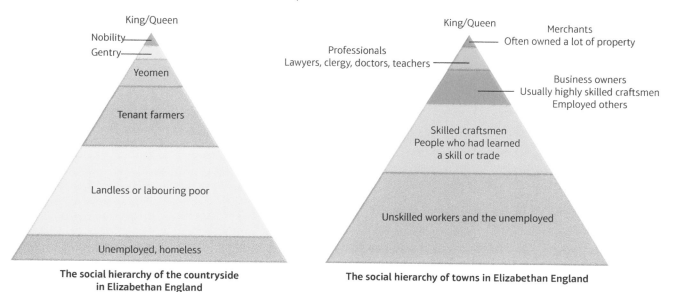

The social hierarchy of the countryside in Elizabethan England

The social hierarchy of towns in Elizabethan England

Figure 1.1: Elizabethan society was a hierarchy in which everyone had a clear place in the social order.

Wherever you were in Elizabethan society, you had to respect and obey those above you and you had to care for those below you. For example, landowners were supposed to take care of their tenants, especially during difficult times.

Households were run along similar lines to society. The husband and father was head of the household. His wife, children and any servants were expected to obey him.

Government

Elizabethan government was made up of the Court, the Privy Council and Parliament. There were also Lords Lieutenants and Justices of the Peace who made sure law and order was kept. The figure below shows how all the different parts of Elizabethan government worked together.

Elizabeth I
The monarch was head of the government.

Justices of the Peace (JPs) and Lords Lieutenants were the most important part of local government*. **Their role was** to make sure government policies were carried out locally and to keep law and order.

The Court was made up of courtiers*. These were nobles and important advisers. The Court had no power but courtiers could influence the king or queen. **Its role was** to entertain as well as advise the monarch.

The Privy Council was made up of 19 Privy Councillors. It met three times a week. Elizabeth was usually in charge of the meetings. **Its role was:**
• to advise the monarch on government policy*
• to carry out the Elizabeth's decisions
• to check what the Justices of the Peace were doing.

Parliament was made up of the House of Lords* and the House of Commons*. The House of Lords was made up of noblemen and bishops. The House of Commons was made up of MPs who were voted for by male landowners.

Its role was:
• to grant extraordinary taxation* if the monarch needed more money
• to pass laws (Acts of Parliament).
You can see what the Elizabethan parliament looked like on page 12.

Figure: Structure of the Elizabethan government.

Key terms

Courtiers*
Men and women of the nobility. Courtiers spent much of their lives with Elizabeth I in court.

Policy*
A plan of action decided on by a government.

House of Commons*
One of the two houses of parliament. The Commons was made up of elected knights and townspeople.

House of Lords*
One of the two houses of parliament. The Lords was made up of the nobility and clergy.

Key terms

Extraordinary taxation*
Occasional, additional taxation to pay for unexpected expenses, especially war.

Local government*
People who run smaller areas and districts of a country.

The monarch

The government in Elizabethan England centred on the monarch. Monarchs of England believed that the right to rule had been given to them by God. This was later known as divine right*. Because of this, Elizabeth I made all the important decisions with the advice of her Privy Council. She could also:

- decide to go to war and make peace
- agree to, or reject, any laws parliament voted for
- make decisions in some law cases, for example, if the law was unclear or if people asked her to change the decision of a judge
- give lands, money and jobs to people.

One of the most important powers Elizabeth had was patronage*. Patronage can be a very effective way of getting support from people and controlling them. However, what the queen gave, she could also take away if she wasn't happy.

The Secretary of State

Elizabeth's most important advisor was her Secretary of State. He advised the queen on what was important to the Crown*. Sir William Cecil (see Source A) was Elizabeth's most successful and important Secretary of State.

Key terms

Divine right*

Belief that the monarch's right to rule came from God.

Patronage*

Giving someone encouragement, wealth or support. For example, Elizabeth gave patronage to explorers. She gave them money for their voyages and praised their efforts.

Crown*

With a capital 'C', the Crown refers to the monarch and his or her government.

Foreign policy*

How one country decides to behave towards another country.

Succession*

Deciding who is going to become king or queen after the monarch dies.

Source A

Sir William Cecil (Lord Burghley from 1571), painted after 1587 by an unknown artist.

The monarch and parliament

When Elizabeth had extra expenses to pay for, such as wars, she had to ask parliament for the money. Because she had to do this, it meant she could not rule without parliament. There were also times when Elizabeth wanted new laws passed. She could issue direct orders but they could not become law without parliament's approval. Although important policies had to be approved by parliament, parliament rarely refused to do this. However, there were some things that only the monarch could decide. Elizabeth I said it was her right to stop parliament talking about:

- foreign policy*
- who she might marry
- who might be monarch next – the succession*.

Extend your knowledge

Elizabethan parliament

Elizabeth's House of Commons was very different from today's House of Commons. There were no political parties and no prime minister, and only wealthy men could vote or become members of parliament (MPs). Candidates for election were chosen by Privy Councillors.

Activity ?

Write a job advertisement for one of the roles in Elizabeth's government, either: a courtier; a Privy Councillor; an MP; a Lord Lieutenant or a JP (see page 10). You should:

a give the job title and who should apply (remember, apart from courtiers, all the jobs were for men only)

b explain what tasks an applicant would need to do and where they would be based

c describe why the job was important to the queen.

Ask a classmate to check the advertisement you have written, and suggest improvements.

Source B

A drawing of Elizabeth I sitting in parliament. It is an English engraving from the 16th century. The queen's importance is shown by the size of her throne.

The Virgin Queen

Legitimacy

To inherit the throne, you had to be legitimate*. Not everyone believed Elizabeth was legitimate because her father, Henry VIII, had divorced his first wife, Catherine of Aragon, in order to marry Elizabeth's mother, Anne Boleyn. The pope, the head of the Roman Catholic* Church, had refused to allow the divorce.

In 1536, Anne Boleyn was executed for treason*. Henry VIII said Elizabeth was illegitimate and could never become queen. He later changed his mind.

Key terms

Legitimate*

Born to parents who are married.

Roman Catholic*

The form of Christianity followed by most people up until the 16th century. The pope was the head of the Catholic Church.

Treason*

Trying to kill the monarch or badly damage the country.

Heir*

Someone who, by law, takes on a title and the property of another person such as king or queen, when that person dies.

Was Elizabeth I legitimate?

Henry VIII needed a son to be king after him. He was married to Catherine of Aragon and they had a daughter, Mary. But it looked as if Catherine couldn't have more children.

Henry wanted a divorce from Catherine so that he could marry Anne Boleyn, who he hoped would give him a son. The pope refused a divorce, so Henry set up his own Church called the Church of England. Then he gave himself a divorce and married Anne.

Many Catholics did not believe Henry had the right to give himself a divorce. They said he was still married to Catherine. When Anne Boleyn gave birth to Elizabeth, they refused to accept that she was legitimate.

Figure: The 'legitimacy' of Elizabeth I.

Gender and marriage

It was unusual, and it was also thought to be unnatural, for a woman to rule as queen. The Christian religion taught that women should obey men. Monarchs were also expected to lead their armies into battle and this would not have been seen as a suitable thing for a woman to do.

Advantage
My husband could lead an army in war, which is an important part of a monarch's role.

Advantage
Having children will make it clear who is the next ruler of England. If there is no heir* people might fight each other for the throne.

Disadvantage
Who would I marry? I am queen, and yet wives are expected to obey their husbands. People might treat my husband as though he had more power than me.

Disadvantage
The only man suitable for me to marry would be a foreign prince, but he would put England's needs second to those of his own country.

Figure: The advantages and disadvantages of Elizabeth marrying.

Women were not thought to be capable of ruling. Even in the home the husband was head of the house. It was unusual for women to be in a position of power.

Many people thought that Elizabeth should marry (see the figure, page 13). However, she did not want to. Elizabeth turned down offers of marriage from:

- her brother-in-law, Philip II of Spain
- King Eric of Sweden
- the heir to the French throne, the Duke of Alençon.

Elizabeth's sister, Mary I, had been England's first queen. Her short reign* convinced many people that women should not rule (see Interpretation 1). While Mary I was queen (1553–58) there had been the following problems.

- Mary's marriage to King Philip II of Spain was so unpopular that it led to a rebellion.
- England joined with Spain in a war against France and lost.
- The Crown had money problems. Many ordinary people were also very poor. There had been several bad harvests leading to disease, hunger and poverty.
- Mary burned to death almost 300 people for their Protestant* beliefs.

Key terms

Reign*

The length of time a king or queen rules a country.

Politics*

How to get, keep and use power.

Protestants*

Protestants were Christians but they did not accept the pope as their religious leader. Nor did they agree with some Catholic teachings.

Stereotype*

An exaggerated idea of what someone or something is like.

Character and strengths

In 1554 Elizabeth had been accused of treason against her sister, Mary I, who was queen. Elizabeth was imprisoned in the Tower of London. This taught her that the court could be a dangerous place, where angering the monarch could get you killed. Courtiers were often involved in plots to gain more power for themselves.

Highly intelligent

Well educated – she spoke Latin, Greek, French and Italian

Excellent grasp of politics*

Could make great speeches and win people over

Confident, with a strong personality

Had a temper that people feared

Often took a long time to make up her mind, which could be frustrating for her advisers

Figure: What was Elizabeth like?

Activities

1 Working in pairs, write a quiz about Elizabeth I. Look back at what you have learned about Elizabeth so far. Think about her character, her powers and the problems she faced as queen.

2 What sort of person would make a successful 16th-century monarch? Draw a crown and around it and write down words to describe what you think would make a good monarch.

3 Did Elizabeth have any of the qualities you identified? Draw a table with two columns, one headed 'Strengths' and the other 'Weaknesses'. Write Elizabeth's strengths and weaknesses in the columns.

Interpretation 1

Historian Christopher Haigh interprets Elizabeth as a strong, independent female leader in the book *Elizabeth I* (1988).

Elizabeth sought [wanted] to present herself, woman though she was, as a fit occupant of the throne of England, and she did not propose [want] to confuse the issue by recruiting [marrying] a husband or an heir. … This was done not by an attack upon the sixteenth century stereotype* of a woman. Elizabeth accepted the image and often derided [made fun of] her own sex… she did not seek to change the ideal [the way women were thought to be], but to escape from it, by suggesting that she was no ordinary woman.

Elizabeth I (1558–1603) at her coronation, painted after 1600 by an unknown artist.

Challenges at home and from abroad

Financial weakness

England's monarchs could not do whatever they pleased. They might rule by divine right, but they needed money and support to rule successfully. Monarchs could raise money from:

- rents and income from their own lands (Crown lands)
- taxes from trade (known as **customs duties**)
- extraordinary taxation agreed by parliament
- profits of justice (fines, property or lands taken from people convicted of crimes)
- loans (sometimes people were forced to lend the government money and were never repaid).

Elizabeth's government did not have a lot of money. England had fought costly wars before Elizabeth became queen and lots of Crown lands had been sold off to raise money to fight them. When she took the throne, the Crown was £300,000 in debt, which was a huge sum in 1558. The Crown usually only earned about £286,667 per year.

To be strong, Elizabeth had to be wealthy. Defending England and keeping her throne was very expensive. Taxes were unpopular and parliament had to agree to them. Elizabeth was worried that if she asked parliament for money they would expect her to do things for them she didn't want to do. She did not, therefore, want to have to rely too much on parliament for her income.

Key term

Ally*

A friend.

The French threat 1558–59

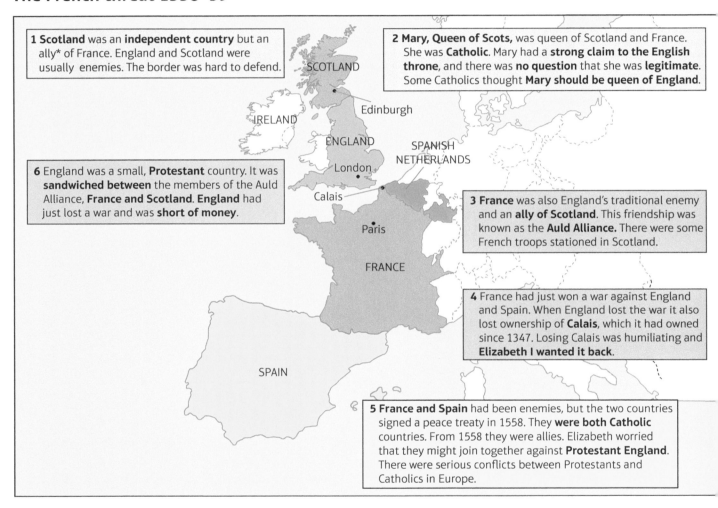

1 Scotland was an **independent country** but an ally* of France. England and Scotland were usually enemies. The border was hard to defend.

2 Mary, Queen of Scots, was queen of Scotland and France. She was **Catholic**. Mary had a **strong claim to the English throne**, and there was **no question** that she was **legitimate**. Some Catholics thought **Mary should be queen of England**.

6 England was a small, **Protestant** country. It was **sandwiched between** the members of the Auld Alliance, **France and Scotland. England** had just lost a war and was **short of money**.

3 France was also England's traditional enemy and an **ally of Scotland**. This friendship was known as the **Auld Alliance.** There were some French troops stationed in Scotland.

4 France had just won a war against England and Spain. When England lost the war it also lost ownership of **Calais**, which it had owned since 1347. Losing Calais was humiliating and **Elizabeth I wanted it back**.

5 France and Spain had been enemies, but the two countries signed a peace treaty in 1558. They **were both Catholic** countries. From 1558 they were allies. Elizabeth worried that they might join together against **Protestant England**. There were serious conflicts between Protestants and Catholics in Europe.

SCOTLAND
IRELAND
Edinburgh
ENGLAND
SPANISH NETHERLANDS
London
Calais
Paris
FRANCE
SPAIN

Figure: The French threat, 1558–59.

Activities

1 Add a section to the quiz which you began on page 14 to test others in your class on foreign threats to Elizabeth I.

2 Give two reasons why each of the following were a problem for Elizabeth:

   a the Crown being in debt

   b Mary, Queen of Scots

   c being a queen in 16th-century England.

3 Look back at the problems in question 2. If you were Elizabeth, which problem would you want to solve first and how would you go about doing it?

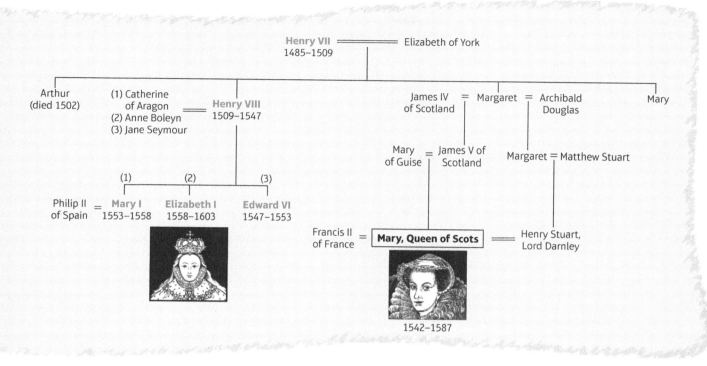

Figure 1.3 Elizabeth I's family tree showing Mary, Queen of Scots' claim to the English throne.

Summary

- Elizabeth I was only England's second ruling queen and it was thought unnatural for women to rule alone.
- Elizabeth was highly intelligent, and confident but could be indecisive.
- Elizabeth was the head of the government and made all the key decisions.
- However, she also needed her Privy Council, parliament, Lords Lieutenants and JPs to govern effectively.
- The monarch decided what the country's religion would be.
- England faced possible threats from France, Scotland and Spain.
- Elizabeth's claim to the throne was doubted by some Catholics who saw her cousin, the Catholic Mary, Queen of Scots, as a possible alternative ruler.

Checkpoint

Strengthen

S1 Give one issue Elizabeth I faced over her suitability to rule England.

S2 Give at least one way in which the Privy Council, parliament and JPs were important in governing England.

S3 Describe two of Elizabeth I's strengths and two of her weaknesses as a monarch.

Challenge

C1 Explain why each of the following were a problem for Elizabeth:
- gender
- foreign policy.

If you are not confident about any of these questions, form a group with other students, discuss the answers and then record your conclusions. Your teacher can give you some hints.

1.2 The 'settlement' of religion

Learning outcomes

- Understand the key features of the English Reformation and religious divisions in England in 1558.
- Understand the key features, and impact, of Elizabeth's religious settlement.
- Understand the role of the Church of England under Elizabeth's rule.

The English Reformation

Religion was central to life in the 16th century. Until 1517, most people in European countries were Catholic. Baptism*, marriage and death were all marked by special services and ceremonies. Confession of sins* and taking part in mass* were vital to keeping your soul from going to hell. Even after you were dead, prayers from others could still help you on your way to heaven. Religion guided people's morals* and behaviour as well as their understanding of the world.

Key terms

Baptism*

A ceremony carried out on a baby or child. It meant the child had become part of the Christian Church.

Confession of sins*

Sins are acts against God's teachings. Confessing your sins means owning up to them to a priest and accepting some kind of punishment.

Mass*

Roman Catholic service at which Catholics are given bread and wine. Catholics believe that this involves a miracle: the bread and wine is turned into the body and blood of Christ.

Morals*

Knowing right from wrong.

The Reformation*

A challenge to the teachings and power of the Roman Catholic Church. This movement is said to have begun in Europe in 1517.

Persecution*

To punish someone for what they believe, or because of their race or gender.

The Reformation* began in Europe because a growing number of people believed that the Roman Catholic Church had become greedy. It no longer represented a truly Christian life: it needed to be changed, or reformed. This led some people, known as **Protestants**, to set up their own Churches, separate from the pope and the Catholic Church.

In the Catholic Church, the Bible was written in Latin. This meant that normal people could not read it, and the only way they could learn about God was directly from the Catholic Church.

Protestants did not agree. They wanted the Bible in their own language, so they could read it themselves. This would limit how much control people like the pope had over normal people.

The English Reformation began in 1532, when Henry VIII created the Church of England.

By 1558, the Reformation in Europe had led to terrible conflict. With the threat from Protestantism, the Roman Catholic Church focused on strengthening the Catholic faith. Many countries were divided, leading to persecution* and even wars over religion.

Source A

The title page of Elizabeth I's personal Bible, given to her in 1568. It was written in English rather than Latin.

The Catholic religion is the one true faith. The Bible must be in Latin. The Church will tell you what to believe and how to behave. You will speak to God through our priests.

The Protestant faith is the true faith. It follows the Bible strictly. For example, we don't have a pope as there isn't a pope in the Bible. The Bible will be in your own language. You can have your own direct relationship with God.

The Catholic faith

1 The Church is a hierarchy. The pope is its head, then cardinals, archbishops, bishops and priests.

2 The Church can forgive your sins if you confess them to a priest.

3 During mass a miracle occurs. The bread and wine become the body and blood of Christ.

4 Priests are special and wear special clothes.

5 Churches are highly decorated in honour of God.

6 Priests cannot marry.

The Protestant faith

1 There is no hierarchy. There is no pope and there are no cardinals, and it is not necessary to have archbishops or bishops.

2 Sins can only be forgiven by God.

3 The bread and wine symbolise the Last Supper* in the Bible. There is no miracle.

4 Priests are not special and should not wear special clothes.

5 Churches are plain and simple so people aren't distracted from God.

6 Priests can marry and have children.

Figure: Differences between the Catholic and Protestant faiths.

Religious divisions in England in 1558

Elizabeth I was a Protestant. However, when she became queen in 1558, most of her subjects were Catholic. Her sister, Mary I, had made England Catholic again.

Religious conflict was spreading through Europe. Elizabeth feared it might reach England, and for good reason. There was a Roman Catholic alternative for the English throne, Elizabeth's cousin Mary, Queen of Scots.

The clergy*

In 1558, most of England's bishops were Catholic. Changing the religion of the country needed an Act of Parliament. The House of Commons would agree with what Elizabeth wanted, but there were lots of Catholic bishops in the House of Lords (see page 10 for more information on the different Houses in Elizabethan

parliament). Although many priests changed their religion to keep their jobs, others were more determined not to give up Catholicism and refused to become Protestant.

Key terms

Last Supper*

The last meal that Christ shared with his disciples (followers). Commemorating it is very important to Christians as it is a reminder that Christ sacrificed his life to save humanity.

Clergy*

Religious officials, such as bishops and priests.

Key term

German states*

Germany did not exist in the 16th century. There were, however, many (usually small) states where German was spoken but they were independent of each other. These states formed part of the Holy Roman Empire (see page 28).

Activity

?

Make suggestions to help Elizabeth change England's religion without causing unrest or rebellion.

Geographical divisions

Parts of England were more Catholic than others. These areas, such as Lancashire, tended to be further from London.

London, East Anglia and the south-east tended to be more Protestant. They had closer links with the Netherlands and the German states* where Protestantism had become popular.

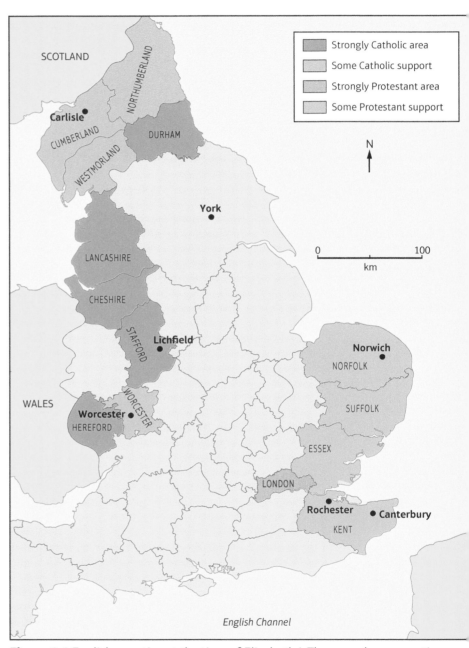

Figure 1.4 English counties at the time of Elizabeth I. The map shows counties that were either strongly Protestant or strongly Catholic or had some support for Catholicism or Protestantism.

Puritans

When Mary I had been queen of England, approximately 300 Protestants were burned for their religious beliefs. Many more escaped into exile* to countries that were more Protestant, such as the Netherlands. They returned to England when Elizabeth became queen. Many were now more committed Protestants with more radical (extreme) beliefs.

Radical Protestants were often known as **Puritans** because they wanted to 'purify' the Christian religion by:

- getting rid of anything that wasn't in the Bible
- having no bishops or pope, or a head of the Church
- having very plain churches – no decoration
- having no special clothes for priests.

Elizabeth's religious settlement, 1559

Elizabeth wanted a compromise* for England's religion. This meant establishing a form of Protestantism that Catholics could accept. Elizabeth did not want a Puritan religion for three main reasons.

Key terms

Exile*

Being made to leave your country as a form of punishment.

Compromise*

An agreement where neither side gets everything they want, but both get some of what they want.

Shilling*

Old money – there were 12 pence to a shilling.

Royal Supremacy*

When the monarch is head of the Church.

Preach*

To speak about religious teachings. A priest would preach in church every Sunday.

Parish*

The area looked after by a priest.

1 It would turn her Catholic subjects against her.

2 Puritans didn't agree with her being head of the Church – this challenged her authority.

3 Elizabeth liked some decoration in churches, and the Puritans were against this.

Features of the religious settlement

Elizabeth I's religious settlement was designed to be accepted by as many of her subjects as possible, Catholic or Protestant. The religious settlement was established in 1559 and came in three parts.

1 **The Act of Supremacy** made Elizabeth the **supreme** governor of the Church of England.

All clergy and royal officials had to swear an oath of allegiance to Elizabeth as head of the Church.

An Ecclesiastical High Commission was set up to enforce the new rules.

2 **The Act of Uniformity** said that all churches and clergy had to follow what the queen wanted so that all churches were **uniform** (did the same thing).

- A new Book of Common Prayer, in English, was published for all clergy to follow. The text was carefully chosen to please Catholics and Protestants.
- The Act described what clothing priests had to wear. The clothing was simpler than Catholics' robes, but was still different to everyday wear.
- Everyone had to go to church on Sunday and other holy days, or they would be fined one shilling*.

3 **The Royal Injunctions** gave further, more detailed instructions on what churches should look like, the clothes priests should wear and what to do in church services. They also said:

- all clergy must teach Royal Supremacy*
- anyone refusing to go to church was to be reported to the Privy Council
- no one was allowed to preach* without a licence from the government
- each parish* was to have a copy of the Bible in English
- images in churches were allowed.

Figure: The religious settlement.

Key terms

Saints*

A saint is someone who lived an exceptional, holy life. To be made a saint by the Catholic Church, several conditions have to be met, including having lived a good life.

Non-conformity*

Doing something different to what is expected.

Fines

If you did not attend church on a Sunday, you could be fined. Although earnings varied widely, the Labourers' Act of 1563 said that:

- labourers could earn up to three pence a day
- skilled craftsmen could earn up to four pence a day
- a servant could earn between eight and nine pence a week.

Therefore, for many people, a fine of a shilling (12 pence) for not attending church on a Sunday, as stated in the Act of Uniformity, could total a week's pay. For the nobility, however, a shilling would not be a serious amount of money.

Images and statues

The Royal Injunctions allowed images in churches. Allowing images meant that the insides of churches remained largely the same, helping to make Elizabeth I's changes less unsettling. Puritans, however, especially disliked saints*' statues, as the Bible forbade worshipping idols. Traditionally, idols were images or representations of gods. Puritans believed people should only pray to God, and that praying to idols was a sin.

Exam-style question, Section B

Describe **two** features of the Elizabethan religious settlement.　　**4 marks**

Exam tip

The answer must give some supporting information for both examples. You will get a mark for each feature, and a mark for supporting each feature with one additional piece of information. Make your points clearly in fully developed sentences and then move on to the next question.

Interpretation 1

Historians Turvey and Heard look at the effectiveness of Elizabeth's settlement in *Change and Protest 1536–88: Mid-Tudor Crises?* (1999).

… the Settlement had mixed success. It largely succeeded in establishing a broadly based national Church which excluded as few people as possible. … On the other hand, the Settlement not only failed to attract the Puritans but… devout [seriously committed] Catholics were likewise marginalised [felt left out] with the consequence of encouraging opposition and non-conformity*.

Key
1. Altar*, which is set apart from the congregation*
2. Priests wore highly decorated robes
3. Painted walls depicting Bible stories
4. Stained glass window
5. Elaborate crucifix* and statues of saints

Figure 1.5 Traditional Catholic church in the reign of Mary I.

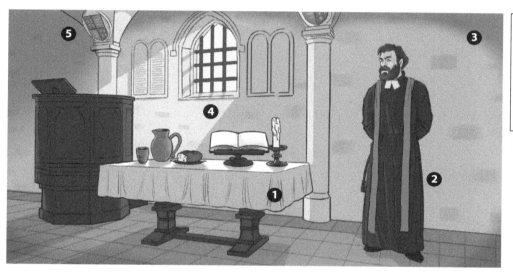

Key
1. Plain table instead of an altar
2. Simple robes
3. No decoration
4. Plain windows
5. Royal crest* instead of religious decoration

Figure 1.6 Protestant church in Elizabethan England.

The impact of the religious settlement

Elizabeth wanted a Protestant Church that Catholics could accept. She did not want them to feel forced to choose between loyalty to their religion and their queen and she didn't want people to be persecuted for their religion. She hoped that the Catholic faith would simply fade away as Catholic priests died. Interpretation 1 (see page 22) sees the Elizabethan religious settlement as successful – up to a point.

The clergy

All members of the Church had to take the oath* of supremacy (under the Act of Supremacy). Eight thousand priests did so, out of approximately 10,000 parishes, showing that the religious settlement was largely successful.

However, only one bishop took the oath. The other 27 were replaced by Protestants.

Key terms

Altar*
Table where mass is celebrated.

Congregation*
The people at a church service.

Crucifix*
Image of Christ dying on the cross.

Royal crest*
The monarch's symbol.

Oath*
A serious promise, usually made on a holy book, like the Bible.

The people

Most Catholics accepted Elizabeth's religious settlement. The wording of the new Prayer Book helped because there weren't too many changes from the Catholic version.

Parishes where Catholics were in the majority were slow to change to the new services. Nevertheless, Elizabeth did not want recusants* punished harshly.

In most places the change of religion went smoothly. However, in some places, such as in London, Protestants violently destroyed Catholic church ornaments and statues of saints.

Key terms

Recusants*

Catholics who were unwilling to attend church services laid down by the Elizabethan religious settlement.

Inheritance*

To come into possession of money, land or other goods from someone else.

Source B

Written by an observer attending an open-air preaching event at Dedham, Essex, in 1575. He describes the impact of the preacher.

… at Dedham men hang weeping on the necks of their horses after Mr. Rogers's sermon [religious teaching] had acted out a little scene in which God threatened to take away the Bible from the English people.

The role of the Church of England

The parish church was a central point of village life. Religion could stir up great emotion (as shown in Source B).

Church courts

The Church had its own courts. Although they were used mainly for Church matters, they did deal with some moral issues like bigamy (being married to more than one person at the same time). Church courts also dealt with wills and inheritance*. For example, the Church courts were in charge of proving a will was valid before anyone could inherit money from it. Lawyers did not like how much power the Church courts had.

All other offences, such as disputes over land, robbery, fraud, rape and murder, were dealt with in the ordinary court system.

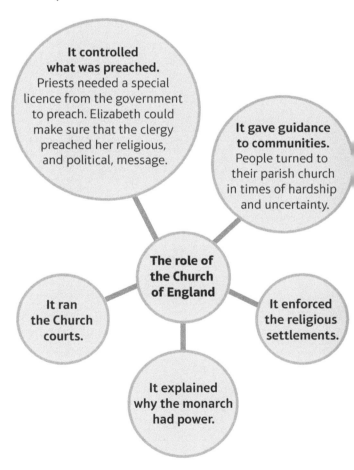

Figure 1.7 The role of the Church of England.

Enforcing the settlement

The Church helped enforce the religious settlement. Visitations were inspections of churches and clergy by bishops to ensure that everyone was following the religious settlement. Clergy also had to show their preaching licences. Elizabeth made it clear that she did not want those carrying out visitations to be too harsh. Even so, the first visitations in 1559 led to 400 clergy losing their jobs.

After 1559, visitations took place every three to four years.

Activities

1 Draw up a table with two columns. Write at the head of the columns: 'Catholic' and 'Protestant'. In each column, list as many features of the religious settlement as you can that:

   a pleased Catholics

   b pleased Protestants.

2 Design a leaflet that tells people, in a clear and helpful way, what they need to know about the religious settlement. Give advice on what they need to do to avoid being fined.

Summary

- Elizabeth was a Protestant queen but England was not a completely Protestant country.
- More Protestant areas of the country were London, the south-east and East Anglia, while Catholicism was especially strong in the north and west of England.
- The religious settlement came in three parts: the Act of Supremacy, the Act of Uniformity and the Royal Injunctions.
- In some places, changing over to the new religious settlement was very slow.
- Visitations enforced the religious settlement but Elizabeth ordered them not to be too harsh.

Checkpoint

Strengthen

S1 What were Elizabeth's main aims in her religious settlement?

S2 What two Acts of Parliament were part of the religious settlement and what did they say?

S3 What were the Royal Injunctions?

S4 In what ways did the Church of England enforce the religious settlement?

Challenge

C1 Do you think Elizabeth's religious settlement:

    • was popular   • was not very popular?

   Try to find some evidence to support each bullet point.

If you are not confident about any of these questions, discuss the possible answers in pairs and then record your conclusions. Your teacher can give you some hints.

1.3 Challenge to the religious settlement

Learning outcomes

- Understand the nature and extent of the Puritan challenge to Elizabeth I.
- Understand the nature and extent of the threat of the Catholic Church, including the Revolt of the Northern Earls.
- Understand the nature and extent of the threat of foreign powers to Elizabeth I.

The nature and extent of the Puritan challenge

Puritans hoped the religious settlement was the start of the Church of England becoming even more Protestant. However, as far as Elizabeth I was concerned, England's religion was settled and things wouldn't change.

It was not long before Puritan clergymen began disobeying parts of the religious settlement. For example, some wanted an end to music in church, or wanted to stop celebrating some holy days. This was a direct challenge to Elizabeth I's authority as Supreme Governor of the Church of England. The two biggest issues were over crucifixes and vestments*.

The crucifix controversy

To Puritans, crucifixes represented idols. However, Elizabeth liked them and she wanted to keep them so as not to alarm Catholics by changing the look of the churches too much. She insisted that each church should display a crucifix. When some Puritan bishops threatened to resign, the queen backed down.

Elizabeth could not enforce her will in this instance. She could not afford to ignore the Puritan bishops' concerns. There weren't enough suitable Protestant clergymen to replace any bishops who were dismissed. Nevertheless, Elizabeth kept a crucifix in the Royal Chapel.

Key term

Vestments*
Special clothes worn by priests.

Source A

Puritan father teaching his family. This woodcut picture was made in 1563.

The vestment controversy

Highly decorated vestments were too Catholic for Puritans. Some thought they should have no special clothing, others that it should be very plain and simple.

The Royal Injunctions said clergy must wear special vestments, but by 1565 it was clear that some were not doing so. In 1566, the Archbishop of Canterbury, Matthew Parker, invited 110 priests to London to show them what they must wear. Thirty-seven refused to attend and they lost their posts. The majority of priests, however, agreed to wear the appropriate vestments, so Elizabeth largely got her way.

The nature and extent of the Catholic challenge

The papacy* and the Counter-Reformation

At this time, the papacy was making new efforts to fight back against Protestantism in Europe. This was known as the **Counter-Reformation**.

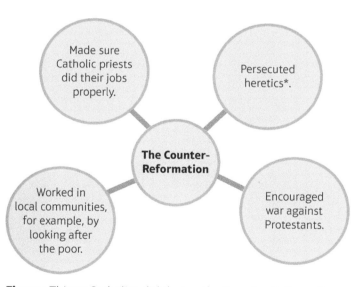

Figure: Things Catholics did during the Counter-Reformation.

The papacy did not do much about England's religious settlement. All the pope did was to say in 1566 that Catholics should not attend Church of England services. People could be fined for this. If they continued to not attend, they could be imprisoned or executed. However, Elizabeth ordered that she did not want recusants punished harshly. She did not want to create martyrs*. As a result, England was stable in the first decade of her reign (see Interpretation 1).

Interpretation 1

From *The Reign of Elizabeth: England 1558–1603*, Barbara Mervyn writes about the effectiveness of Elizabeth's religious policies (2001).

By 1568, Elizabeth's policies seemed to be working. The early problems caused by the settlement seemed to be fading. The majority of Catholics outwardly conformed [went along with it in public] and, without any leadership from the Pope, were politically loyal.

England's nobility and the Catholic threat

It is difficult to know how acceptable ordinary English Catholics found the Elizabethan Church. However, approximately one-third of the nobility and many gentry were recusants, especially in the north and north-west of England.

In November 1569, the Catholic earls of Northumberland and Westmorland led a rebellion in the north of England against Elizabeth. It is known as the Revolt of the Northern Earls (see Chapter 2).

The rebels marched south. By 22 November, they controlled a large amount of land in the north-east of England. One of the key events of the rebellion was the taking of Durham Cathedral and the celebration of a full Catholic mass at the cathedral.

The earls of Northumberland and Westmorland asked the Catholic nobility to join them, but most refused and stayed loyal to Elizabeth. Only the Duke of Norfolk (Elizabeth's distant cousin) was part of the plot.

Elizabeth doesn't listen to Catholics like Mary I did. No one listens to us at Court. Our Protestant queen prefers new, Protestant nobles like Dudley, Earl of Leicester and Sir William Cecil.

Earl of Westmorland

People in the north of England would support us. They are mainly Roman Catholics and want a return to Catholicism.

Earl of Northumberland

Figure: Why the Catholic earls of Northumberland and Westmorland rebelled.

The rebellion was successfully stopped by royal troops. Elizabeth had hundreds of rebels executed, which showed how dangerous she thought the rebellion was. It also changed Elizabeth's relationship with Catholics living in England.

Foreign powers

England was not the only place in Europe where Protestantism was taking root. It was growing in Scotland, France, parts of the Holy Roman Empire* and the Netherlands (which belonged to Spain). However, Catholic powers in Europe were determined to stop Protestantism spreading. Spain, Austria and the Holy Roman Empire were all controlled by members of the Catholic Habsburg family.

France

In 1562 religious war broke out in France. Elizabeth I agreed to help French Protestants. She wanted Calais in return. She had already successfully helped Scottish Protestant lords to rebel against Catholic rule in 1560 (see page 32). This time, however, she failed. The French Protestants made peace with their government without Elizabeth's help.

Key term

Holy Roman Empire*

A large group of different states and kingdoms covering a large area of central Europe, including much of modern Germany and parts of Poland and Austria.

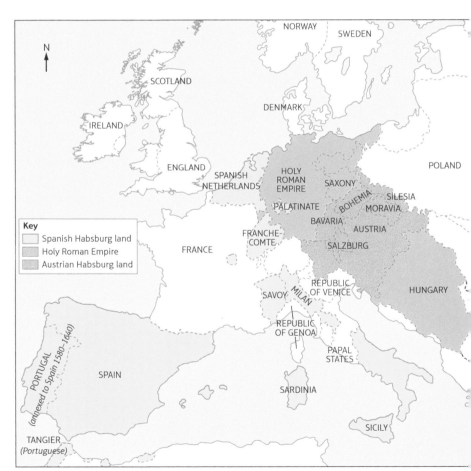

Figure 1.8 Europe during Elizabeth's reign.

Elizabeth's failure in France led to:

- Elizabeth signing the Treaty of Troyes, which said that Calais belonged to France
- Philip II of Spain being angered, as Elizabeth had supported foreign Protestants.

Spain and the Spanish Netherlands

In the 16th century, the Netherlands belonged to the Spanish king, Philip II. He was a strict Roman Catholic and was increasingly annoyed at Elizabeth helping Protestant rebels in France and Scotland. Elizabeth, meanwhile, was concerned that Spain and France might form a Catholic alliance against England. In the 1530s, Pope Paul III had excommunicated* Henry VIII and had then asked France and Spain to invade England and depose him.

In 1563, Philip II banned the import* of English cloth into the Netherlands. So Elizabeth I stopped all English trade with the Netherlands. This was bad for both countries and the bans only lasted a year.

Key terms

Excommunicated*

A very severe punishment, imposed by the pope, expelling people from the Catholic Church.

Import*

Letting foreign goods into your country.

Spanish Inquisition*

A religious court set up by Spain to keep Spanish territories true to the Catholic faith. Anyone caught not following Catholic teachings by the Inquisition could be tortured or publicly burned alive.

The Dutch Revolt

1566: The Dutch Revolt begins
- Philip II decides to reorganise the Dutch government and sends the Spanish Inquisition* to crush Protestantism in the Netherlands.
- Philip's actions are unpopular and the Dutch rebel.

1567: Philip sends the Duke of Alba to the Netherlands
- Alba, a Spanish general, arrives in the Netherlands with an army of 10,000 men.
- Alba sets up a Council of Troubles to restore order and enforce Spanish Catholic rule. Thousands are killed (mainly Protestants).

1567–68: Elizabeth takes action
- Elizabeth lets Dutch Protestant refugees come to England.
- Some Dutch rebels, called the Sea Beggars, attack Spanish ships in the English Channel.
- Elizabeth allows the Sea Beggars to shelter in English ports.
- 1568: Spanish ships carrying gold that Philip has borrowed from Genoa (in Italy) shelter from a storm in an English port.
- Elizabeth takes the gold. She says it is Genoa's money, not Philip's. Philip is furious.

1568: The Dutch Revolt is crushed
In 1568 the Dutch Revolt is defeated but Alba's army stays in the Netherlands.

Figure: Events in the Netherlands, Spain and England 1566–69.

...n is a great Catholic power. It ...ts to destroy Protestantism. ...must stop this happening.

Alba's army is a real threat to England. And thousands of Protestants are being killed. We must help Dutch Protestants.

What is England going to do then, Your Majesty?

I understand but I cannot afford a war against Spain – or worse, against Spain and France together.

I agree, but I do not want to be seen as Europe's leading Protestant monarch. Getting involved in a religious war in the Netherlands could lead to a religious civil war in England.

I shall try to make things as difficult as possible for Spain in the Netherlands without getting involved directly.

Figure: William Cecil and Elizabeth I discussing the problem of Spain in the Netherlands.

Source B

Colour engraving from 1567 showing the Spanish Inquisition arriving in the Netherlands. The Duke of Alba established a Council of Troubles to persecute not only rebels but also heretics. Hundreds were killed.

Activities ?

1 Look at Source B. Why would pictures such as this have worried Elizabeth I and her Privy Council? Why might they be especially concerned in 1568?

2 Write a narrative account of what happened during the Dutch Revolt. Try to include as much detail as you can, including what Elizabeth did to help Dutch Protestants.

What was Elizabeth trying to achieve?

Elizabeth was trying to protect her throne and avoid war. By making things difficult for Spain she hoped Spanish forces would simply leave the Netherlands. Her strategy was risky. It became riskier still in 1568–69 for two main reasons.

1 In 1568, Mary, Queen of Scots, fled to England from Scotland (see page 32). Many Catholics believed she had a stronger claim to the throne than Elizabeth I.

2 The Revolt of the Northern Earls happened in 1569 (see Chapter 2). Although it failed, it encouraged Philip II to support further plots against Elizabeth I. He could use Alba's army in the Netherlands against her.

Activities

1 After reviewing the section 'The nature and extent of the Catholic challenge', find a blank piece of paper. Draw a line down the centre of it to make a timeline of Catholic threats to Elizabeth I. On one side of the line put threats from home and the dates, and on the other put foreign threats and the dates. Check you have the threats in the correct order. What do you notice about the Catholic threat to Elizabeth I in the 1560s?

2 The main foreign Catholic challenges to England in the 1560s came from France and the Spanish Netherlands. Look back at page 29 and decide which you think was the greater threat to Elizabeth.

Summary

- Challenges to the religious settlement came from both at home and abroad.
- In England, the Catholic challenge to the religious settlement was limited until 1569.
- The Puritans challenged both the use of crucifixes and vestments.
- Elizabeth sent troops and financial assistance to deal with the Catholic challenge to Protestants in Scotland (1560) and France (1562) but did not do so for the Dutch (1566).
- England's relations with Spain got much worse after the Dutch Revolt began.
- The Dutch Revolt caused concern to England because of the large Spanish army sent to the Netherlands to put it down and crush Protestant heresy.
- By sheltering the Sea Beggars and seizing gold bullion from Philip II's ships, Elizabeth hoped to make it too difficult for Spanish forces to remain in the Netherlands.

Checkpoint

Strengthen

S1 Describe the crucifix and vestments controversies and their outcomes.

S2 Give two reasons why the Catholic threat in England was not serious until 1569.

S3 What was the Dutch Revolt about and why was Spain involved?

S4 Give two reasons why the Dutch Revolt worried Elizabeth so much.

S5 Give two examples of things Elizabeth did that annoyed Spain.

Challenge

C1 Explain why Elizabeth intervened to help Protestants in France but not in the Netherlands.

For these questions, it might be helpful to draw a timeline of events. Having a visual representation of the period may make things clearer when writing your answers.

1.4 The problem of Mary, Queen of Scots

Learning outcomes

- Understand why Mary, Queen of Scots, had a claim to the English throne.
- Understand the relationship between Mary, Queen of Scots, and Elizabeth I between 1568 and 1569.
- Examine the evidence for and against Mary, Queen of Scots' accusation of murder.

Timeline

Mary, Queen of Scots

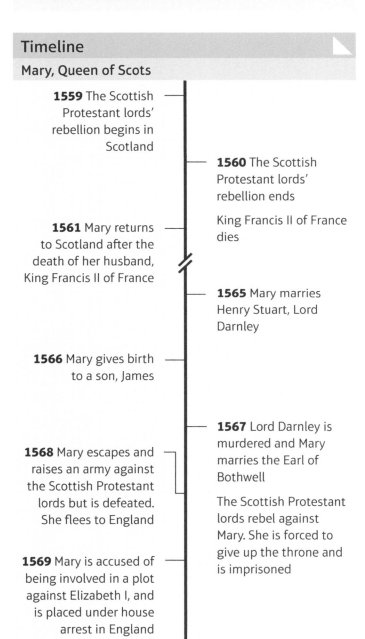

1559 The Scottish Protestant lords' rebellion begins in Scotland

1560 The Scottish Protestant lords' rebellion ends

King Francis II of France dies

1561 Mary returns to Scotland after the death of her husband, King Francis II of France

1565 Mary marries Henry Stuart, Lord Darnley

1566 Mary gives birth to a son, James

1567 Lord Darnley is murdered and Mary marries the Earl of Bothwell

The Scottish Protestant lords rebel against Mary. She is forced to give up the throne and is imprisoned

1568 Mary escapes and raises an army against the Scottish Protestant lords but is defeated. She flees to England

1569 Mary is accused of being involved in a plot against Elizabeth I, and is placed under house arrest in England

Mary, Queen of Scots' claim to the English throne

Mary, Queen of Scots, was a Catholic with a strong claim to the English throne (see page 17). Her great-grandfather was the English king, Henry VII. Her father was James V of Scotland and her mother was Mary of Guise, who was from a powerful French, Catholic, noble family.

Mary, Queen of Scots, became queen of Scotland at six days old after her father, James V, died. She married King Francis II of France in 1558, and lived in France with him until he died two years later. At one point, Mary was both Queen of Scots and the queen of France.

The Treaty of Edinburgh, 1560

In 1559, Scotland's Protestant lords rebelled because they did not like being ruled by a French, Catholic queen. They asked Elizabeth I for help. She was not keen to help with getting rid of a fellow monarch. However, she knew that, with French help, Mary, Queen of Scots, could take her throne. Elizabeth therefore secretly sent money and troops to help the rebels.

The successful rebellion was ended by the Treaty of Edinburgh in 1560. The Protestant lords took over Scotland. When Mary, Queen of Scots, returned there after the death of her husband in December 1560, she was queen but it was the Protestant lords who controlled the Scottish government.

The Treaty of Edinburgh said that Mary would give up her claim to the English throne, but Mary herself never agreed to the treaty. She wanted to be named as Elizabeth's heir.

Even though Elizabeth had helped the Protestant lords to rebel, Mary still thought that Elizabeth should make her heir to the English throne. Elizabeth could have done this. However, she decided this would only encourage Catholics to plot against her, knowing that Mary would be the next queen. It would also have been very unpopular with Protestants in England who did not want a Catholic monarch.

Key term

Abdicate*

A king or queen giving up their throne.

Mary, Queen of Scots' arrival in England, 1568

Mary married her second husband, Henry Stuart, Lord Darnley, in 1565. She gave birth to their son, James, in 1566. In 1567, Darnley was murdered and Mary was suspected of being involved.

The Protestant lords rebelled again and forced Mary to abdicate*. She was imprisoned but escaped in 1568. She raised an army to win back her throne but her forces were defeated. Mary fled to England, hoping for Elizabeth I's help against the rebels.

Source A

A 16th-century Scottish painting of Mary, Queen of Scots (right), and her husband, Henry Stuart, Lord Darnley. Lord Darnley was Mary's distant cousin and also descended from King Henry VII, so he too had a claim to the English throne.

Relations between Elizabeth and Mary, 1568–69

What were Elizabeth's options?

Mary arrived in England in May 1568. She wanted Elizabeth's help. Elizabeth could not decide if she should help or not. She did not approve of lawful monarchs being overthrown, but Mary was a threat to her. Elizabeth ordered that Mary be held under guard until she had made up her mind. Elizabeth's options are shown in the figure opposite.

Activities ?

1 Imagine you are Elizabeth I. List the advantages and disadvantages of the four options for what to do with Mary.

2 If you were Elizabeth I, which option would you choose and why? Write a short letter to your Secretary of State, Sir William Cecil, explaining your decision.

3 Split into two groups, with one group arguing for Mary being allowed to stay in England, and the other group against. Have a debate. Make sure you include all the information you listed in your advantages and disadvantages list.

Elizabeth and Mary never met, but they did exchange letters. Mary had asked for a meeting with Elizabeth to persuade her that she was innocent in the murder of her husband, Lord Darnley. Her request was refused.

A court heard the case against Mary for the murder of Lord Darnley between October 1568 and January 1569. Mary said the court had no right to try a queen. She wanted Elizabeth to promise that the court would say she was innocent. Elizabeth refused.

Key term

Deposed*

When a king or queen is removed from power.

Option 1: Help Mary regain her Scottish throne

Problem: This would mean supporting a Catholic against Protestants.

Option 2: Hand Mary over to the Scottish Protestant lords

Problem: Mary would be deposed*, helped by Elizabeth. This would not set a good example because the same thing could happen to Elizabeth.

Option 3: Allow Mary to go abroad

Problem: Mary could get support from Catholic France and/or Spain to regain her throne – and possibly take Elizabeth's throne from her.

Option 4: Keep Mary, Queen of Scots, in captivity in England

Problem: She could be a focus of Catholic plots against Elizabeth I as long as she was alive.

Figure: Mary, Queen of Scots – was she guilty or not guilty?

Guilty or not guilty?

The court could not decided whether Mary was guilty or not guilty. Mary therefore stayed in England, in captivity. She remained a threat to Elizabeth, as Interpretation 1 shows.

Interpretation 1

Historian Susan Brigden discusses the threat of Mary, Queen of Scots, in her book, *New Worlds, Lost Worlds* (2000).

Whether in England or in Scotland or in France, Mary posed a perpetual [constant] menace, for she always pressed [continued making] her claim to the English throne, and sought [looked for] by any means to free herself from a protection which became captivity.

THINKING HISTORICALLY **Cause and Consequence (4a&b)**

Fragile history

Nothing that happens is bound to happen. Sometimes things happen due to the actions of an individual or chance events that no one expected. Something could have changed or someone could have chosen differently, bringing about a very different outcome.

Work on your own and answer the questions below. When you have answered the questions, discuss the answers in a group. Then have a class vote.

Possible reasons why Elizabeth I successfully established her religious settlement

| Elizabeth I's strategy to make her religious settlement acceptable to both Catholics and Protestants. This is called the middle way. | Growth of Protestantism in England | Recusants were not treated harshly | Visitations to enforce Elizabeth's religious settlement | The decision to keep Mary, Queen of Scots, in captivity in England | Catholic Spain and France did not unite against Protestant England | Elizabeth I not getting directly involved in the Dutch Revolt |

1 Think about Elizabeth I's middle way strategy.
  a How did not treating recusants harshly affect the success of Elizabeth I's middle way strategy?
  b If recusants had been treated harshly, would the middle way strategy have worked?
2 Think about Elizabeth's motivations.
  a What might have happened if Elizabeth I had decided to take military action to support the Dutch rebels?
  b Would all the other reasons why her religious settlement was successful have worked?
  c What might have happened if Spain and France had united against England?
  d How did keeping Mary, Queen of Scots, in captivity in England make a difference?
3 Write down any reasons why the Elizabethan religious settlement was successful that could be called 'chance events'. How important were these in the success of the Elizabethan religious settlement?
4 Imagine you are alive in November 1558, when Elizabeth I became Protestant queen of a country that was still largely Roman Catholic. Write a paragraph explaining what you think might happen over the next 11 years. Do you think she will be able to keep it Protestant?
5 Have a class vote. Was the success of Elizabeth I's religious settlement bound to happen? Be prepared to back up your decision.

Exam-style question, Section B

Explain why the Catholic threat to Elizabeth I increased after 1566.

You may use the following in your answer:
- the Dutch Revolt
- Mary, Queen of Scots' arrival in England in 1568.

You must also use information of your own. **12 marks**

Exam tip

Don't just describe events. You must focus on reasons for the Catholic threat against Elizabeth becoming more serious.

Activity ?

Create a spider diagram showing the reasons why Elizabeth was so careful when making a decision about the fate of Mary, Queen of Scots.

Plot and rebellion, 1569

Not only would Elizabeth not name an heir, she refused to discuss marriage. In 1569, a plot was planned by courtiers which aimed to deal with the problem of Mary and the succession. The plan was to marry Mary to the Duke of Norfolk, who was a Protestant, so any children would be Protestant too, and they would have a strong claim to the throne. Mary liked the plot.

The Earl of Leicester eventually told Elizabeth of the plan. It showed how dangerous Mary was. Nevertheless, Elizabeth still refused to take any strong action against Mary.

Summary

- Mary, Queen of Scots (Elizabeth's second cousin), is **NOT** Queen Mary I (Elizabeth's sister).
- The arrival of Mary, Queen of Scots, in England was a huge problem for Elizabeth I.
- Mary had a strong claim to be next in line to the English throne after Elizabeth.
- Mary became the focus of a plot at court in 1569 to marry her to the Duke of Norfolk.
- The plot to marry Mary to the Duke of Norfolk was developed into a rebellion by the Catholic earls of Northumberland and Westmorland.
- Elizabeth did not want to take action against Mary because she was an anointed monarch.
- From 1568, Mary remained in captivity in England.

Checkpoint

Strengthen

S1 Describe the chain of events that led Mary, Queen of Scots, to come to England.

S2 Give two options Elizabeth had in dealing with Mary and say why she did not take them.

S3 What was the aim of the plot concerning Mary that developed at court?

Challenge

C1 Explain how changes in Scotland caused problems for Elizabeth I.

If you are not confident about constructing answers to these questions, write a list of all factors related to the problems described, using information from the chapter to help you. This will help to structure your answer.

Recap: Queen, government and religion, 1558–69

Recall quiz

1 What were the key features of the Privy Council?
2 What were the three key parts of Elizabeth's religious settlement?
3 Give two ways in which the religious settlement was enforced.
4 Which parts of England had the most Catholic support during Elizabeth's early reign?
5 Give three pieces of evidence that show the religious settlement wasn't accepted by everyone.
6 In what year did the Dutch Revolt begin?
7 Which treaty was signed in 1560? What was the main aim of the treaty?
8 Who was Mary, Queen of Scots, accused of murdering?
9 Give two reasons why Elizabeth needed to keep Mary, Queen of Scots, in captivity.
10 Who plotted to become Mary, Queen of Scots' husband?

Exam-style question, Section B

'Religion was Elizabeth's main problem in the years 1558-69.' How far do you agree? Explain your answer.

You may use the following in your answer:

- the settlement of religion
- Mary, Queen of Scots' arrival in England in 1568.

You must also use information of your own. **16 marks**

Exam tip

You will have to decide if you think religion was 'the **main** problem' Elizabeth had. To do this, explain why religion was a serious problem. Then choose two other problems Elizabeth I faced and explain why they were serious problems too. In your conclusion, you should compare the three problems and explain which you think was most serious and why.

Activity

How successful was Elizabeth's first decade of rule? Write a report of how you think Elizabeth did.

This will come in three sections:

- a The settlement of religion
- b Religious challenges
- c The problem of Mary, Queen of Scots.

In pairs, for each of these sections, make a list of ways she was successful and ways she wasn't. Did things work out as she hoped? Were there any failures or mistakes?

Now for each section give Elizabeth a score on the following scale:

- 1 = Complete failure.
- 2 = Largely a failure.
- 3 = Largely a success.
- 4 = Complete success.

Under each heading, write the score you are giving Elizabeth and a short sentence to explain why.

- d Draw up a list of Elizabeth's strengths and weaknesses in 1569. Look at the table you drew for strengths and weakness on page 14. Are there any differences?
- e If there are differences – which differences show Elizabeth had become stronger and which show Elizabeth had become weaker?

Writing historically: managing sentences

Successful historical writing is clearly expressed, using carefully managed sentence structures.

Learning outcomes

By the end of this lesson, you will understand how to:

- select and use single clause and multiple clause sentences.

Definitions

Clause: a group of words that contains a verb, and can form part or all of a sentence, e.g. 'Elizabeth I reigned over England from 1558'.

Single clause sentence: a sentence containing just one clause, e.g. 'Elizabeth I reigned over England from 1558.'

Multiple clause sentence: a sentence containing two or more clauses, often linked with a conjunction, e.g. 'Elizabeth I reigned over England from 1558 and was known as 'The Virgin Queen'.'

Co-ordinating conjunction: a word used to link two clauses of equal importance within a sentence, e.g. 'and', 'but', 'so', 'or', etc.

How can I structure my sentences clearly?

When you are explaining complicated events and ideas, you can end up writing very long sentences. These can make your writing difficult for the reader to follow.

Look at the extract below from a response to this exam-style question:

> Describe **two** features of the Revolt of the Northern Earls.   (**4 marks**)

> *England was a Protestant country but the Northern Earls and their followers aimed to bring back Catholicism in England so they began a revolt and at the beginning of the revolt they took control of Durham Cathedral and celebrated mass there.*

1. The writer of the response above has linked every piece of information in his answer into one, very long sentence.

    How many different pieces of information has the writer included in this answer? Rewrite each piece of information as a **single clause sentence**. For example:

> *The Northern Earls wanted England to be Catholic.*

2. Look again at your answer to question 1. Which of the single clause sentences would you link together? Rewrite the response twice, experimenting with linking different sentences together using **conjunctions** such as 'and', 'but' or 'so'. Remember: you are aiming to make your writing as clear as possible.

How can I use conjunctions to link my ideas?

There are several types of **multiple clause sentence** structures that you can use to link your ideas.

If you want to balance or contrast two ideas of equal importance within a sentence, you can use co-ordinating conjunctions to link them.

Look at the extract below from a response to this exam-style question:

> Explain why the Catholic threat to Elizabeth I increased after 1566.
>
> **(12 marks)**

> Mary, Queen of Scots, arrived in England in 1568. Because she was a Catholic and had a link to the English throne, with the support of France, many saw her as a Catholic alternative to Elizabeth. This not only worried Elizabeth, but also gave many the chance to plot against her whilst Mary was close by. Mary kept up her claim for the English throne, not face to face with Elizabeth but through letters, as Elizabeth refused to meet her in person.

These co-ordinating conjunctions link equally important actions that happened at the same time.

These paired co-ordinating conjunctions contrast two different things.

These paired co-ordinating conjunctions link and balance two equally important ideas.

3. Experiment with rewriting some or all of the response, using different sentence structures and different ways of linking ideas.

Improving an answer

4. Now look at the final paragraph below, which shows the response to the exam-style question above.

> After 1566, Elizabeth faced threats from many different Catholic enemies. Mary, Queen of Scots, served as a constant reminder that she was a Catholic alternative to the Protestant Elizabeth. With this threat so close to home, plots were easily started. The Revolt of the Northern Earls was not a revolt of ordinary Elizabethan people. Many high-ranking members of the nobility were involved. Elizabeth could not underestimate these Catholic threats.

Rewrite this paragraph, choosing some conjunctions from the **Co-ordinating Conjunction Bank** below to link, balance or contrast the writer's ideas.

Co-ordinating Conjunction Bank	
and	not only... but also...
but	either... or...
or	neither... nor...
so	both... and...

02 | Challenges to Elizabeth at home and abroad, 1569–88

Elizabeth I faced many serious threats between 1569 and 1588, both from within England and from abroad.

One threat was the plot to replace Elizabeth with Mary, Queen of Scots. This plot involved Catholics in England supported by Spain and France.

Roman Catholic priests were smuggled into England from Europe to keep the Catholic faith alive. This resulted in more plots against Elizabeth.

Another challenge faced by Elizabeth was the Netherlands. England's increasing involvement in the Netherlands angered Philip II of Spain, as the Netherlands was under Spanish rule.

Events in the 'New World' were also challenging. Europeans had only been aware of the Americas since 1492. By the time of Elizabeth's reign, Spain had many settlements there. English ships, led by people like Sir Francis Drake, tried to disrupt Spanish trade and to set up English colonies, further annoying Philip II of Spain.

By the mid-1580s, England and Spain were at war, despite Elizabeth's efforts to avoid it. Philip planned an invasion of England, and in 1588 he launched his Armada.

Learning outcomes

By the end of this chapter, you will:

- understand the plots against Elizabeth I and know how the Elizabethan government was able to defeat these threats to the queen
- know and understand the key events that brought about the worsening of Anglo–Spanish relations, 1569–88
- understand why Mary, Queen of Scots, was finally executed in 1587
- understand why events in the Netherlands were so important to the security of England
- understand why Philip II sent the Armada against England in 1588 and why it failed.

By the end of the 1560s Elizabeth I faced many threats to her throne, both at home and from abroad. Figure 2.1 highlights the main threats Elizabeth faced at the beginning of the 1570s.

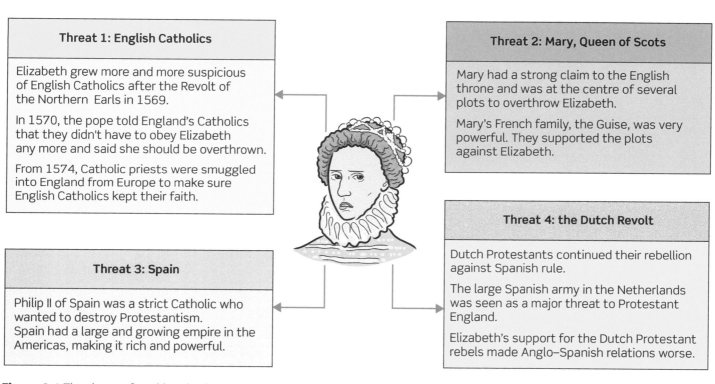

Threat 1: English Catholics

Elizabeth grew more and more suspicious of English Catholics after the Revolt of the Northern Earls in 1569.

In 1570, the pope told England's Catholics that they didn't have to obey Elizabeth any more and said she should be overthrown.

From 1574, Catholic priests were smuggled into England from Europe to make sure English Catholics kept their faith.

Threat 2: Mary, Queen of Scots

Mary had a strong claim to the English throne and was at the centre of several plots to overthrow Elizabeth.

Mary's French family, the Guise, was very powerful. They supported the plots against Elizabeth.

Threat 3: Spain

Philip II of Spain was a strict Catholic who wanted to destroy Protestantism.
Spain had a large and growing empire in the Americas, making it rich and powerful.

Threat 4: the Dutch Revolt

Dutch Protestants continued their rebellion against Spanish rule.

The large Spanish army in the Netherlands was seen as a major threat to Protestant England.

Elizabeth's support for the Dutch Protestant rebels made Anglo–Spanish relations worse.

Figure 2.1 The threats faced by Elizabeth I at the start of the 1570s.

The Revolt of the Northern Earls, 1569

Most people living in the north of England, including the northern noble families, were Catholic. Elizabeth I made England Protestant. She gave new, Protestant nobles from the lower ranks of the nobility important roles in her government. In 1569, Elizabeth faced a serious threat when some northern earls led Catholic northerners in a rebellion against her.

Why did the northern earls revolt in 1569?

The following factors came together and led to the Revolt of the Northern Earls in 1569.

- The earls wanted England to return to being Catholic.
- The earls had lost their influence at court after Elizabeth I became queen and they weren't happy about this.
- Elizabeth refused to name an heir or to marry.
- Mary, Queen of Scots, in captivity in England, could potentially replace Elizabeth and, in doing so, resolve the other issues the earls had.

Who were the key players in the Revolt of the Northern Earls?

Mary, Queen of Scots
- She wanted to be queen of England.
- Agreed to marry the Duke of Norfolk.
- If they had children, her children would be heirs to the English throne.

Earl of Northumberland
- Was Catholic and had lost the power he once had at court.
- Elizabeth had also taken away his rights to a copper mine on his land.

Ordinary northerners
- Strongly Roman Catholic so wanted the return of Catholicism.
- They hated the new, Protestant archbishop of Durham, who was trying to force the North to become Protestant.

Activity ?

How many different reasons can you find to explain why the Northern Earls' Rebellion took place?

Key term

Civil war*
A war between people of the same country.

Earl of Westmorland
- Was Catholic and had lost the power he once had at court.

Duke of Norfolk
- Said he was Protestant but had close links with the northern Catholic families.
- Coming from an ancient family, he particularly hated Elizabeth's new ministers, such as William Cecil.
- If he married Mary, Queen of Scots, and she became queen, he would rule England and their children would become heirs to the throne.

Protestant courtiers
- Wanted an heir to the throne to avoid a possible civil war* when Elizabeth died.
- Supported the possible marriage between Mary, Queen of Scots, and the Duke of Norfolk. Norfolk was Protestant, so they expected children from the marriage would be Protestants too.

Figure: Reasons for the Revolt of the Northern Earls.

One of the main parts of the Revolt of the Northern Earls was the plan to marry Mary to the Duke of Norfolk. The plan was not treason, but there were problems with it.

- Marriage between members of the nobility needed the queen's approval.
- Elizabeth had made it clear that she alone would decide her successor.
- The Duke of Norfolk had Catholic sympathies, so England might end up with a Catholic monarch.

Source A shows that Mary's motives were already more ambitious than just marrying Norfolk. It also shows that the Spanish ambassador to Elizabeth's court was involved in the plot. In fact, Mary had received word that Spain would provide troops to help with the rebellion.

Source A

A letter to Philip II written by Guerau de Spes, Spain's ambassador to Elizabeth's court, on 8 January 1569.

The Queen of Scotland told my servant to convey [say] to me the following words: – 'Tell the ambassador that, if his master will help me, I shall be Queen of England in three months and mass shall be said all over the country'.

Plan for the Revolt of the Northern Earls, November–December, 1569

1. *The earls of Northumberland and Westmorland will raise rebel forces in the north of England and take control of Durham.*

2. *The rebels will then march south towards London to join with the Duke of Norfolk.*

3. *Several thousand Spanish troops will land in Hartlepool to support the rebel forces.*

4. *The Duke of Norfolk and the rebel forces will seize control of the government in London and overthrow Elizabeth I.*

5. *Any resistance will be overthrown by the Spanish troops.*

6. *Meanwhile, Mary, Queen of Scots, is to be freed, ready to marry the Duke of Norfolk and take the English throne.*

Figure 2.2 The plans made by northern earls for their revolt, 1569.

The key events of the revolt

- Elizabeth's courtiers develop a plot to marry Mary, Queen of Scots, to the Duke of Norfolk. Their children could be heirs to the English throne.

↓

- As the plot develops, the Earl of Leicester gets cold feet. Leicester decides to tell Elizabeth about the plot.

↓

- Elizabeth has the Duke of Norfolk arrested.
- The earls of Northumberland and Westmorland panic but decide to go ahead with the rebellion.

↓

The plot goes ahead. Durham is taken by the rebels and they celebrate mass in Durham Cathedral. The northern earls now control much of the North of England.

↓

Elizabeth sends the Earl of Sussex to put down the rebellion. He has 14,000 troops. There are only about 5,400 rebels. Spanish help never arrives. The rebels flee.

↓

- Elizabeth executes 450 rebels in towns and villages across the north.
- The Earl of Westmorland escapes but the Earl of Northumberland is captured and executed.
- The Duke of Norfolk is released from prison.
- Mary, Queen of Scots, is moved further south, to Coventry.

Figure: How the Revolt of the Northern Earls developed.

Although Elizabeth acted harshly towards most rebels, she did not execute Norfolk or Mary, Queen of Scots. Mary had been overthrown in Scotland by rebels. If Elizabeth had executed her it would look as though she supported the rebels. As a queen herself, Elizabeth did not agree with monarchs being overthrown or executed.

Parliament and the Privy Council were frustrated by Elizabeth's lack of action.

The failure of the plot led the pope to issue a papal bull* in 1570, urging all loyal Catholics to overthrow Elizabeth. He hoped to encourage a new rebellion.

In response in 1571, laws were passed in England saying it was treason* to say Elizabeth I was a heretic*, or that she was not the queen. It also became treason to have papal bulls printed or circulated in England.

Figure 2.3 shows how the rebellion was a real threat to Elizabeth. Even though the revolt had failed, it showed there was still lots of Catholics in the country who wanted Protestantism gone from the country. While the revolt was taking place, mass was celebrated at churches across the north-east of England.

Key terms

Papal bull*

A written order issued by the pope.

Treason*

Doing something that threatens the country or the leader of the country.

Heretic*

People with beliefs different to those of the rest of society and especially those against the teachings of the Catholic Church.

Activity ?

Study Figure 2.3. Which three points in the revolt do you think would have given Elizabeth I most cause for concern? Why?

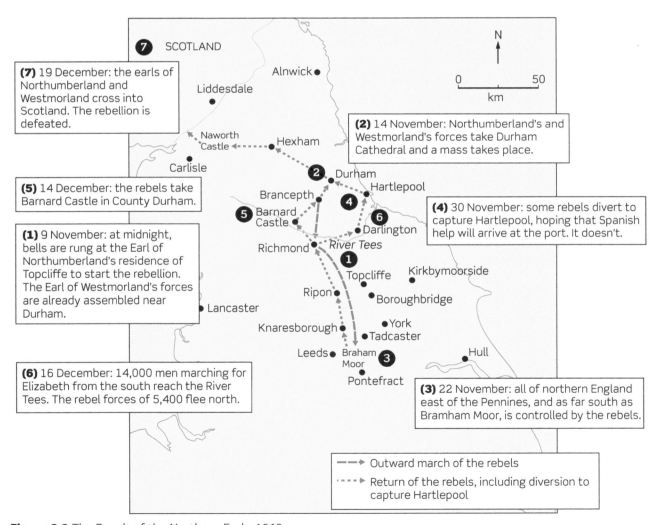

(7) 19 December: the earls of Northumberland and Westmorland cross into Scotland. The rebellion is defeated.

(2) 14 November: Northumberland's and Westmorland's forces take Durham Cathedral and a mass takes place.

(5) 14 December: the rebels take Barnard Castle in County Durham.

(4) 30 November: some rebels divert to capture Hartlepool, hoping that Spanish help will arrive at the port. It doesn't.

(1) 9 November: at midnight, bells are rung at the Earl of Northumberland's residence of Topcliffe to start the rebellion. The Earl of Westmorland's forces are already assembled near Durham.

(6) 16 December: 14,000 men marching for Elizabeth from the south reach the River Tees. The rebel forces of 5,400 flee north.

(3) 22 November: all of northern England east of the Pennines, and as far south as Bramham Moor, is controlled by the rebels.

- - -► Outward march of the rebels

· · · ·► Return of the rebels, including diversion to capture Hartlepool

Figure 2.3 The Revolt of the Northern Earls, 1569.

The significance of the Revolt of the Northern Earls

Figure: The significance of the Revolt of the Northern Earls.

The significance of the papal bull

The papal bull issued by the pope put England's Catholics in a difficult position.

- Did they obey the head of their Church?
- Or did they obey their queen?

This direct order was issued by the pope made it impossible to be loyal to both the Catholic Church and the crown. It meant that now all English Catholics were under suspicion of treason.

The Ridolfi, Throckmorton and Babington plots

The Ridolfi plot, 1571

1 Ridolfi was a banker but he was also an Italian spy living in England and working for the pope. In 1571, he developed a plot to get rid of Elizabeth. In the plot, the Duke of Norfolk would marry Mary, Queen of Scots, and Spain would invade England. Mary would be made queen of England.

2 Ridolfi met the pope, Philip II of Spain and the Duke of Alba in the Netherlands. He had a letter from the Duke of Norfolk. Norfolk said he would lead a rebellion against Elizabeth if Philip agreed to send Alba and 10,000 Spanish troops to help.

3 Sir William Cecil uncovered the plot. Norfolk was executed in 1572. Elizabeth refused to take action against Mary. However, Ridolfi was abroad when the plot was discovered and he escaped.

Figure: The Ridolfi plot.

Showed there was still a threat from Spain because the Duke of Alba had been involved.

Showed there was still a threat from Catholics and Mary, Queen of Scots.

Why the Ridolfi plot was important

Because of the threat from Spain, Elizabeth realised she had to make relations with France better.

Figure: Significance of the Ridolfi plot.

45

Priests and priest holes

To support English Catholics, Catholic priests were smuggled into England from 1574. They travelled undercover, staying with rich Catholic families, where they held services. Catholic homes were regularly raided where priests were thought to be staying. Priests who were caught risked being hanged, drawn and quartered*. In many homes, secret hiding places called priest holes were made (see Source B).

Key terms

Hanged, drawn and quartered*

A type of punishment used when the accused was found guilty of high treason. The accused would be hanged until nearly dead, then cut open to have their intestines removed, and finally chopped into four pieces.

Recusants*

Catholics who refused to go to Protestant church services.

Source B

A raid on a Catholic house in Northamptonshire, described by a Catholic priest, John Gerard, who was staying there. He managed to hide in the priest hole without being caught.

There they were, straining and shouting to get through and search the house, yet they halted in an unlocked room just long enough to allow us to reach the hiding-place and shut ourselves safely in. Then they... burst into the lady's apartment while others raged round the remaining rooms.

In 1581, parliament passed two laws against Catholics.

- Recusants* would be fined £20 – an enormous sum that would bankrupt most families.
- Anyone caught trying to convert people to Catholicism would be tried for treason.

Actions taken against English Catholics were becoming harsh, but the plots against Elizabeth continued. The figures opposite show what happened in two important plots against Elizabeth – the Throckmorton plot and the Babington plot.

The Throckmorton plot, 1583

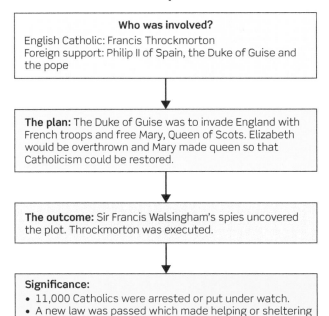

Figure: The Throckmorton plot.

The Babington plot, 1586

Figure: The Babington plot.

Mary, Queen of Scots' execution

Why was Mary, Queen of Scots, executed?

Elizabeth hesitated to execute Mary, but eventually signed the order for her death in February 1587. Mary, Queen of Scots, had been involved in plots before, so why was she executed in 1587?

1   A new law had been passed in 1585: The Act for the Preservation of the Queen's Safety. It said that Mary would not be allowed to inherit the throne if Elizabeth was assassinated. It also said that Mary could be executed if a proper trial was held and she was found guilty of plotting against Elizabeth. The letters Mary wrote to Babington were enough evidence to find her guilty.

2   By 1586, Elizabeth knew that Philip II of Spain was planning to attack England with an Armada*. In January 1587 there were rumours that Spanish troops had already landed in Wales. These rumours made it clear to Elizabeth that she had to get rid of Mary before the Spanish really did try to invade.

Exam-style question, section B

Describe **two** features of the plots against Elizabeth I in the years 1571–86.   **4 marks**

Exam tip

This question is worth only 4 marks. Although 4 marks can make a difference to your overall result, you should only spend about 4–6 minutes on it. This means you must be very clear and concise.

Key term

Armada*
A fleet of ships.

Source C

Painted c1613. The execution of Mary, Queen of Scots, at Fotheringhay Castle on 8 February 1587.

What was the significance of Mary, Queen of Scots' execution?

The execution of Mary, Queen of Scots, removed an important threat to Elizabeth I. However, Philip II had been planning to invade England since 1585. Mary's execution gave him another reason to want to remove Elizabeth.

Activity ❓

Review the plots against Elizabeth I. Draw and fill in a table with four columns: **Plot name and date, Who was involved?; The basic plan;** and **Outcomes**.

Walsingham's use of spies

In 1573, Sir Francis Walsingham became Elizabeth I's Secretary of State. He was vital in uncovering plots against Elizabeth I.

Walsingham used spies to uncover plots (see the figure below). Many Catholic priests who were captured were executed. During Elizabeth I's reign, 130 priests and 60 of their supporters were executed.

Key terms ◣

Pardon*

Being forgiven for a crime and let off punishment.

Cipher*

A secret way of writing in code.

Agents provocateurs*

French term referring to agents who become a part of groups suspected of wrongdoing, and encourage other members to break the law so that potential threats can be identified and arrested.

Source D ◣

Sir Francis Walsingham in a letter to Lord Burghley (William Cecil) in 1575. He was writing about trying to stop the plots surrounding Mary, Queen of Scots.

Without torture I know we shall not prevail.

Activity ❓

Work in pairs. Discuss the following statement: 'Francis Walsingham is one of England's unknown heroes.'

   a One person notes down evidence supporting this statement and the other notes down evidence against it. Write up your evidence together in one paragraph.

   b Join with another pair. Each person reads out their argument and listens carefully to everyone else's. Take a vote on whether you agree with the statement or not.

Who were the spies?
- The spies were specially trained agents who tracked suspects such as Catholic priests. Walsingham had spies in France, the German states, Spain and other countries, as well as in England.
- Ordinary people were also paid for useful information.
- Sometimes Catholic priests who had been captured would spy or give information in return for a pardon*.

Sir Francis Walsingham and his spy network

What did the spies do?
- They used ciphers* to hide plans.
- They let plots develop to get enough evidence against people, e.g. Mary, Queen of Scots.
- Agents provocateurs* were used to stir up trouble and trap people.
- Torture was used if it was the only way to get information out of someone. See Source D.

Figure: How Sir Francis Walsingham used spies.

THINKING HISTORICALLY ▶ Cause and Consequence (3a&b)

We all make decisions, whether they turn out to be right or wrong

1 Work in pairs.

Describe to your partner a situation where things did not work out as you had planned. Then explain how you would have done things differently to achieve a better result. Your partner will then tell the group about that situation and whether they think that your alternative actions would have been better.

2 Work individually.

a Write down what the Duke of Norfolk's aims were in his plans to marry Mary, Queen of Scots, in 1569.

b Write down what the Duke of Norfolk's actions were and for each one list at least one consequence of the action.

c How successful was the Duke of Norfolk in achieving his aims?

d Think about what effect the Duke of Norfolk's actions had on the future lives of English Catholics. Were they good for English Catholics or were they bad?

3 Do you think the Duke of Norfolk knew what might happen? If you were the Duke of Norfolk, what would you have done differently? Discuss these questions with a partner and decide whether you think people in history are in control of the history they make.

Summary

- The Revolt of the Northern Earls in 1569 was a serious rebellion focused on overthrowing Elizabeth I and restoring Catholicism.
- Elizabeth I's excommunication in 1570 put English Catholics in a difficult position between loyalty to their political leader, Elizabeth I, or their spiritual leader, the pope.
- Plots against Elizabeth were encouraged by Spain and the pope.
- Three other plots aiming to replace Elizabeth I with Mary, Queen of Scots, were: Ridolfi (1571); Throckmorton (1583); and Babington (1586).
- Mary, Queen of Scots, was executed in 1587 after the Babington plot.
- Plots against Elizabeth failed because Sir Francis Walsingham had an extensive network of spies and informers.
- Catholic priests were smuggled into England to support English Catholics.

Checkpoint

Strengthen

S1 Give two pieces of evidence of each of the following factors in causing the Revolt of the Northern Earls in 1569.

    a Political factors   **b** Religious factors

S2 Give one important outcome for each of the plots against Elizabeth I: the Revolt of the Northern Earls; the Ridolfi plot; the Throckmorton plot and the Babington plot.

S3 Give three reasons why Sir Francis Walsingham's spy network was so effective.

Challenge

C1 Compare the threats to Elizabeth I between 1571 and 1586. Which do you think was the most serious and why?

If you are not confident about any of these questions, your teacher can give you some hints.

2.2 Relations with Spain

Learning objective

- Understand Elizabeth I's foreign policy aims, and how that affected relations with Spain.

Timeline

The decline in Anglo–Spanish relations, 1570–84

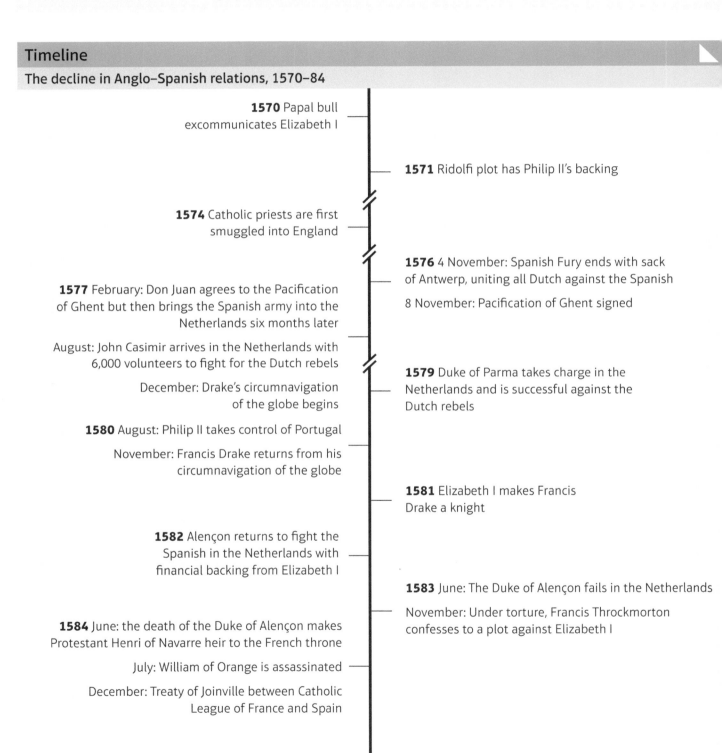

1570 Papal bull excommunicates Elizabeth I

1571 Ridolfi plot has Philip II's backing

1574 Catholic priests are first smuggled into England

1576 4 November: Spanish Fury ends with sack of Antwerp, uniting all Dutch against the Spanish

8 November: Pacification of Ghent signed

1577 February: Don Juan agrees to the Pacification of Ghent but then brings the Spanish army into the Netherlands six months later

August: John Casimir arrives in the Netherlands with 6,000 volunteers to fight for the Dutch rebels

December: Drake's circumnavigation of the globe begins

1579 Duke of Parma takes charge in the Netherlands and is successful against the Dutch rebels

1580 August: Philip II takes control of Portugal

November: Francis Drake returns from his circumnavigation of the globe

1581 Elizabeth I makes Francis Drake a knight

1582 Alençon returns to fight the Spanish in the Netherlands with financial backing from Elizabeth I

1583 June: The Duke of Alençon fails in the Netherlands

November: Under torture, Francis Throckmorton confesses to a plot against Elizabeth I

1584 June: the death of the Duke of Alençon makes Protestant Henri of Navarre heir to the French throne

July: William of Orange is assassinated

December: Treaty of Joinville between Catholic League of France and Spain

Elizabeth I's foreign policy aims

Elizabeth I was in charge of England's foreign policy*. Success in foreign affairs was not easy because:

- England was smaller and poorer than Spain and France
- there were tensions in England between Protestants and Catholics.

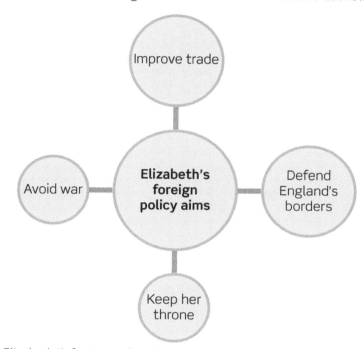

Figure: Elizabeth I's foreign policy aims.

Key terms

Foreign policy*

How a nation deals with other nations. Foreign policy can focus on defending what a country has (a defensive policy) or conquering other lands (an aggressive policy).

New World*

North and South America.

Privateer*

Individuals with armed ships that captured other ships for their cargoes. Privateers often had support from their government.

Merchant*

Someone who buys and sells goods.

Commercial rivalry: the New World*, privateers* and Drake

During Elizabeth I's reign, English merchants* began to explore new places to trade in Europe, Asia and the New World. However, English merchants faced problems in developing trade because Spain controlled:

- the Netherlands, England's main route into European markets and beyond
- much of the New World.

Spain claimed much of the Americas as its own, where vast profits could be made from crops such as tobacco and sugar cane, and from mining silver. However, anyone who wanted to trade there needed a licence from Spain. These were very hard to come by. Many English merchants ignored Spain's rules and traded without licences. Some of them even attacked Spanish ports and shipping.

Activity ?

Francis Drake features strongly in the following sections of this book. As you find out more about him, consider Interpretation 1 (page 52). You could do some more research on Drake, and on the New World trade, too. For example, at this time, Europeans, including Drake, became involved in the African slave trade.

Elizabethans treated Drake like a hero. As you work through this chapter and find out more about Drake, make a list of reasons why Drake would not be thought of as a hero today.

Francis Drake

Francis Drake was a famous English merchant who made his fortune in the New World. He also made huge sums of money for people who invested* in his voyages, including Elizabeth I. However, Philip II saw Drake as a pirate because he stole cargo from Spanish ships.

Key terms

Invested*

Put money into a business or event in return for a share of the money made.

Circumnavigate*

To travel all the way around the world.

Interpretation 1

Historian Angus Konstam talks about Francis Drake in *The Great Expedition* (2011).

… in 1586 England had a national hero who seemed capable of achieving anything he wanted. The boost to national morale was incalculable [enormous]. As the prospects [chance] of war loomed [grew] ever larger, at least England could count on men like Sir Francis Drake to protect them from the wrath [anger] of the Spanish. The irony [strange thing] … is that if anyone helped bring about this war, it was Drake himself.

1. In **1572**, Elizabeth I hired Drake as a privateer. Drake went to Panama, where he captured £40,000 of Spanish silver. This made Philip II very angry. Elizabeth was secretly very pleased with what Drake had done but backing him risked war with Spain.

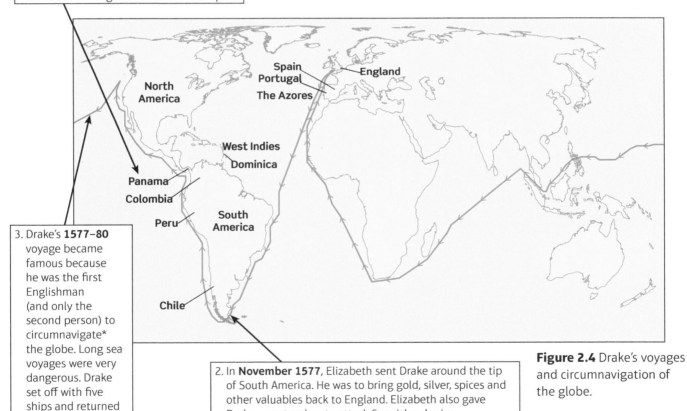

3. Drake's **1577–80** voyage became famous because he was the first Englishman (and only the second person) to circumnavigate* the globe. Long sea voyages were very dangerous. Drake set off with five ships and returned with only one, the *Golden Hind*.

2. In **November 1577**, Elizabeth sent Drake around the tip of South America. He was to bring gold, silver, spices and other valuables back to England. Elizabeth also gave Drake secret orders to attack Spanish colonies.
By **1577**, Anglo–Spanish relations were poor and it was feared Spain might invade England. Elizabeth wanted to weaken Spain by attacking colonies, and make England richer.

Figure 2.4 Drake's voyages and circumnavigation of the globe.

Source A

From an account of Elizabeth I's meeting with Francis Drake before he set sail in 1577.

I would gladly be avenged on the King of Spain for diverse injuries [various insults] that I have received.

The outcome and significance of Drake's voyage

Activities

1. Create a timeline of events for Drake, 1570–80, showing the dates of his voyages.

2. Examine the significance of Drake's actions. Discuss with a partner which you think is the most significant for Elizabeth's relations with Spain.

3. Write a short paragraph explaining your answer.

The voyage resulted in:
- Drake attacking Spanish ports and ships in the Pacific
- Drake claiming an area of north California for England, called **New Albion**
- Drake returning home with £400,000 of Spanish treasure, which was divided between Drake, his investors and Elizabeth
- Elizabeth knighting* Drake.

For Elizabeth it gave her:
- a new colony in the New World
- her cut of the £400,000 in plunder
- more strength politically, and showed Philip II that England would not give in to Spain.

For Drake it made him:
- a national hero
- very rich
- a knight.

For Spain there was:
- anger that Drake was knighted
- the loss of valuable treasure
- challenge to its control of the New World.

Figure: The outcome of Drake's circumnavigation of the globe.

Key terms

Knight*

Knighting someone is a way that the monarch can show that they value and honour a person. Knights are addressed as 'Sir'.

Alliance*

An agreement between two countries.

Political and religious rivalry

In the 1500s, more land meant more people, wealth and power. European nations competed for land. This often led to war.

Religious differences also led to war. Catholics and Protestants each thought the other was wrong, and dangerous.

Nations also made alliances* with each other. Alliances were broken when they were no longer helpful. Spain and England had traditionally been allies. Now England was Protestant, that began to change.

In the 1500s, England was not as wealthy or powerful as Spain and France. Luckily, Spain and France were rivals. This was helpful to Elizabeth I. It meant that Spain and France each wanted England as an ally.

- France wanted England as an ally because it was surrounded by Spanish territory (see Figure 1.8 on page 28).
- Spain wanted England as an ally because English ships could help protect its ships as they sailed past England to the Netherlands.

From 1567, however, Spanish ships were sailing to the Netherlands with resources for the Duke of Alba's army. The Duke of Alba's Spanish army was brutally persecuting Dutch Protestants. Elizabeth's Privy Council wanted her to help the Dutch Protestant rebels.

What did Elizabeth I do about the Netherlands?

Elizabeth I was not keen to help Dutch Protestant rebels in the Netherlands. She wanted to avoid doing anything that could lead to war with Spain (see Figure 2.5).

Instead, she put pressure on the Spanish to encourage them to leave the Netherlands alone. Until 1566, the Netherlands had accepted Philip II as king, but had had a lot of freedom from Spanish control. Elizabeth wanted to go back to this arrangement.

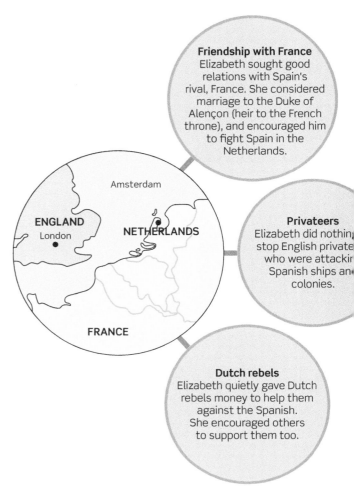

Figure: How Elizabeth put pressure on Spain to leave Dutch Protestants alone.

Figure 2.5 Reasons why Elizabeth I was reluctant to help Dutch Protestant rebels directly.

The Spanish Fury and the Pacification of Ghent, 1576

By 1576, the cost of the war in the Netherlands was too much for Spain. After months without pay, Spain's forces mutinied*, attacking and stealing from Dutch civilians and sacking* the town of Antwerp. This was known as the Spanish Fury. All Dutch provinces*, Catholic and Protestant, united against Spain and drew up a list of demands known as the **Pacification of Ghent**. It said:

- all Spanish troops must leave the Netherlands
- the Netherlands must run its own affairs once more
- the persecution of Protestants must end.

In February 1577 a new Spanish commander called Don Juan arrived in the Netherlands. He agreed the Pacification of Ghent. It looked as though Elizabeth's aims had been achieved.

Key terms

Mutiny*
When soldiers or sailors rebel against their officers.

Sacking*
To rob a town using violence and causing a lot of damage.

Provinces*
Different regions that make up a country.

Source B

Engraving showing mutinying Spanish troops sacking Antwerp in 1576. It was made by the Dutch artist Franz Hogenberg in 1576.

Als man die Spaniard die vberhandt
Namen, die Stat auch sehr verbrant
Den Schis auch ferbt der burger blut

Das karmen in dieser grosser not
Elendigklich war anzusehen
Da von nit muglich war zu fliehen

Seint jung vnd alt beid man vnd weib
Allein zu rretten ir leib
Gefallen in der Statt graben

Vnd so da durch hinaus gewaden
Doch seind auch vil hie blieben todt
Die all verloren leib vnd guth.

Anno Dnj.
M. D. LXXV
·IIII· Nouembr

A missed opportunity?

The figure below shows what happened after the Pacification of Ghent in 1576.

> Soon after the signing of the Pacification of Ghent, Philip II sent a new Spanish army to attack the Netherlands.

> Elizabeth I asked a mercenary*, John Casimir, to gather 6,000 English and Scottish volunteers help the Dutch rebels against the Spanish. By using mercenaries and volunteers, Elizabeth wasn't sending an official English army to fight Spain.

> Casimir's Protestant forces attacked Catholic churches in the Netherlands, angering Dutch Catholics.

> Dutch Catholics made peace with Philip II of Spain because they were upset about their churches being destroyed by Casimir. This weakened the Dutch rebels.

> In 1578, the Dutch were doing well in the war and Elizabeth's Privy Councillors tried to persuade her to send a proper army to the Netherlands to help them. Elizabeth took a long time to decide.

> While Elizabeth was deciding, the Dutch asked France to help. The Duke of Alençon agreed to help and fought the Spanish.

> However, by 1579, the Duke of Parma was in charge of Spanish forces in the Netherlands. He was a better military leader and Spain soon regained control.

Figure: Events in the Netherlands.

Key term

Mercenary*

A soldier who fights for money rather than a nation or cause.

Activity ?

Work in pairs. One of you must decide how far Spain's improving position in the Netherlands in 1579 was a result of Elizabeth I's mistakes. The other must decide how far it was down to factors beyond her control. Compare findings. Make a joint decision about how far Elizabeth I was to blame. Use a value continuum like the one below to illustrate your answer.

100% Elizabeth's mistakes   100% beyond her control

The international situation in 1578	The international situation in 1579
• Spain was financially weak.	• Spain was still financially weak.
• France and England were allies.	• France and England were still allies.
• Don Juan's Spanish army was not very successful.	• Don Juan was replaced by the Duke of Parma. Spain began beating the Dutch.
• Protestant and Catholic Dutch were united under their leader, William of Orange.	• The southern Dutch Catholic provinces made peace with the Spanish.
• The Duke of Alençon led an army into the Netherlands to fight the Spanish.	• The Duke of Alençon withdrew from the Netherlands.

Spain's fortunes restored, 1580–84

In 1580, Philip II managed to gain Portugal plus its colonies and navy. This made Spain even stronger than before and further alarmed Elizabeth, making her even more reluctant to directly help the Dutch. Instead she gave the Duke of Alençon £70,000 to take a French army to the Netherlands. He did so in 1582 but failed again to defeat the Spanish.

Interpretation 2 sees Elizabeth herself as the key reason for her foreign policy's failure.

Interpretation 2

An extract about Elizabeth's involvement in the Netherlands from *Elizabeth I: Meeting the Challenge, England 1541–1603* (2008) by John Warren.

… nothing Elizabeth had done had contributed towards a successful resolution [end] [in the Netherlands] in line with English interests. Instead, she had managed to alienate [upset] Spain without earning the trust of the Netherlands. The unhappy prospect of a complete Spanish victory loomed.

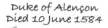

 Duke of Alençon
Died 10 June 1584

 William of Orange
Assassinated 10 July 1584

The deaths of the Duke of Alençon and William of Orange caused problems for Elizabeth's foreign policy because:

- Elizabeth could no longer ask the Duke to fight the Spanish in the Netherlands
- although France's new heir to the throne was Henri of Navarre, a Protestant, leading French Catholics formed a Catholic League who signed an alliance with Spain, called the **Treaty of Joinville**. The alliance aimed to get rid of Protestantism in France.

- it showed how easy it was for a leader like Elizabeth to be assassinated
- Dutch Protestants needed a leader and looked to Elizabeth. She did not want this role as she could be seen as trying to overthrow Philip II
- without a leader, the Dutch rebels could be defeated by Spain, leaving England as Philip II's next target.

Figure 2.6 The impact of the deaths of the Duke of Alençon and William of Orange on Elizabeth I's foreign policy.

1584: a turning point in Anglo-Spanish relations

Summer 1584

The Duke of Alençon has died (June 1584) and William of Orange has been assassinated (July 1584). The Dutch rebels are looking to me for leadership. But sending an army to the Netherlands is too risky. England doesn't have the resources to fight Spain, especially now that Philip II controls Portugal.

We no longer have France as an ally. If the Dutch are defeated, France and Spain may attack Protestant England next. It seems I have run out of options.

End of 1584

France and Spain have signed the **Treaty of Joinville**, and promised to work together to stamp out Protestantism. The defeat of the Dutch rebels is now only a matter of time.

The situation is serious. We must help the Dutch rebels. If we don't, they could be crushed and, if they are, England could be next.

Figure: Elizabeth and Sir William Cecil discuss what to do about Anglo-Spanish relations

Exam-style question, Section B

'The decline in Anglo–Spanish relations in the years 1569–85 was caused by Elizabeth I.' How far do you agree?

You may use the following in your answer:

- Drake's voyages to the New World
- the Netherlands.

You **must** also use information of your own.

16 marks

Exam tip

Planning your answers is a very important part of exam success.

This question tests how well you can explain why something happened but you need to focus on Elizabeth I's role. Analyse how Elizabeth's actions made relations with Spain worse. Then try to analyse two other factors that also worsened relations. For better marks you must provide information of your own. To do this, you **must** take time to plan.

Activities

1 Explain the importance of the following events.
   a The Spanish Fury and Pacification of Ghent.
   b The deaths of Alençon and William of Orange.
2 Why did Elizabeth hesitate in 1584–85 over whether to help the Dutch?

Summary

- Relations with Spain worsened between 1569 and 1585.
- Elizabeth I's foreign policy was defensive – she wanted to avoid war.
- The Dutch Revolt led to a large Spanish military force being sent to the Netherlands. It was seen as very threatening to England.
- English support for Dutch rebels was limited and indirect until 1585.
- Elizabeth I used friendship with France as well as mercenaries to support the Dutch rebels.
- Sir Francis Drake made Philip II angry with his actions in the New World.
- Members of Elizabeth I's Privy Council were frustrated by her hesitation, especially in 1578.
- In 1584, circumstances beyond Elizabeth I's control finally led to her intervening directly in the Netherlands in 1585.

Checkpoint

Strengthen

S1 Give two aims of Elizabeth I's foreign policy.

S2 Write a sentence explaining the importance of the following events in worsening Anglo–Spanish relations 1569–84.
   a Francis Drake's expeditions to the New World.
   b The Dutch Revolt in the Netherlands (including the Pacification of Ghent in 1576).

S3 Elizabeth I tried to avoid direct conflict with Spain but still indirectly put pressure on Spain to leave the Netherlands alone. Describe, and give examples, of two ways in which she did this.

Challenge

C1 Write a paragraph explaining why Anglo-Spanish relations became worse after 1580.

C2 Explain why Elizabeth I knighted Francis Drake in 1581. You must refer to both what he had achieved, and the circumstances the queen faced, by 1581.

To help with these questions, you might find it useful to draw a timeline dating the important moments in Anglo-Spanish relations in the 1570s and 1580s.

2.3 Outbreak of war with Spain, 1585–88

- Understand how England's involvement in the Netherlands encouraged war with Spain.

England's direct involvement in the Netherlands 1585–88

How and why did Elizabeth I change her foreign policy?

After the Treaty of Joinville (see Figure 2.6 on page 57) was signed in 1584, Elizabeth could not avoid getting directly involved in the Netherlands.

Elizabeth takes direct action, 1585

In the summer of 1585, the Dutch Protestants asked Elizabeth to be their queen. She refused because it would mean deposing King Philip II, who was a fellow monarch. She did, however, sign the Treaty of Nonsuch with them. It said England would send an army of 7,400 to the Netherlands to support the Dutch Protestant rebels. This meant that England and Spain were now at war.

In October 1585, Elizabeth also sent Drake to raid Spain's New World territories. She wanted to make it difficult for Philip to get resources from his colonies. Drake's raids made Philip so angry that by the end of the year he had decided to invade England.

Robert Dudley in the Netherlands, 1585–87

Source A

A picture of Robert Dudley, Earl of Leicester, painted in 1585.

Elizabeth sent Robert Dudley, the Earl of Leicester, to command England's forces in the Netherlands. Leicester was not very successful. He only managed to slow the Spanish army's advance through the Netherlands, and prevent them taking the important port of Ostend. The Earl of Leicester's campaign in the Netherlands was not successful for a number of reasons.

Resources
- Leicester was not given enough men or supplies to achieve much.

Why the Earl of Leicester failed in the Netherlands

Trust
- Elizabeth was never fully behind the rebels because she still hoped to negotiate with Spain. The Dutch didn't like this lack of commitment.
- Two English officers defected* to the Spanish, handing over a Dutch town they were guarding. This damaged relations between Leicester and the Dutch leaders.

Different aims
- Elizabeth wanted the Netherlands to stay Spanish, but for the Dutch to be allowed their old freedoms to govern themselves.
- Leicester wanted to free the Netherlands from Spanish control completely.

Figure: Reasons why the Earl of Leicester failed in the Netherlands

Key term

Defected*

Changed sides in a war.

Drake singes the King of Spain's beard, 1587

Since January 1586, Spain had been preparing a large fleet of ships – the Armada. In March 1587, Elizabeth ordered Francis Drake to attack Spain's navy in Cadiz, Spain's most important Atlantic port. Drake destroyed 30 ships and lots of the fleet's supplies. The attack on Cadiz became known as the '**singeing* of the King of Spain's beard**'.

Drake then spent several weeks attacking the coast of Portugal before heading to the Azores. His aim was to capture Spanish treasure ships bringing silver from Spain's New World colonies. Spain had to break off from building the Armada to defend itself against Drake. This delayed the Armada by a year and gave England more time to prepare.

Key term

Singeing*
Burning slightly.

Activity ?

Draw a table with three columns like the one shown below. In each column, list as much evidence as you can to show how each of the three factors led to the decline in Anglo–Spanish relations 1585–88. Two have been entered to start you off.

Politics	Religion	Role of individual
New World colonies – Spain and England competing for territory		Francis Drake – attacked Spanish ships

Summary

- Elizabeth I promised to help the Dutch and signed the Treaty of Nonsuch in 1585.
- However, England's army in the Netherlands was not very successful.
- The Earl of Leicester made little progress in the Netherlands as he did not have enough men or resources.
- Elizabeth sent Sir Francis Drake to raid Spanish New World settlements in 1585.
- In 1587, Drake 'singed the King of Spain's beard' and delayed the launch of the Armada.

Checkpoint

Strengthen

S1 What did Elizabeth I agree to do on signing the Treaty of Nonsuch?

S2 Give two reasons why the Earl of Leicester failed in the Netherlands.

S3 Give two events where Francis Drake angered Philip II and two in which he helped England after 1585.

Challenge

C1 How much was Elizabeth to blame for the Earl of Leicester's failure in the Netherlands?

These questions ask you to take into consideration not just things in this section, but everything you have learned in Chapter 2 so far. If you are struggling, review your notes from the previous sections of this chapter.

2.4 The Armada

Learning objectives

- Understand why Philip II launched the Armada.
- Understand the reasons why the Armada was defeated, and consequences of this English victory.

Why did Philip II launch the Spanish Armada?

Mary, Queen of Scots' execution in 1587 is often thought to be the cause of the launch of the Spanish Armada. However, the decision was actually taken as early as October 1585.

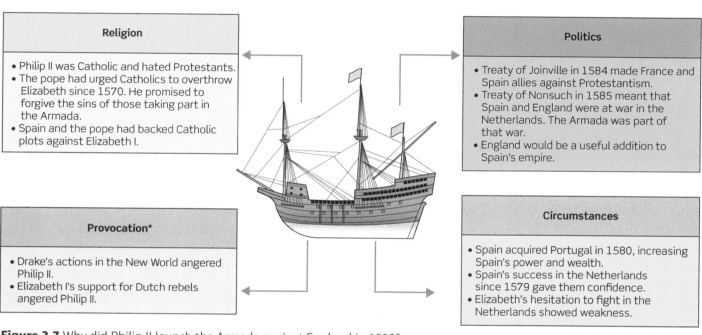

Religion

- Philip II was Catholic and hated Protestants.
- The pope had urged Catholics to overthrow Elizabeth since 1570. He promised to forgive the sins of those taking part in the Armada.
- Spain and the pope had backed Catholic plots against Elizabeth I.

Politics

- Treaty of Joinville in 1584 made France and Spain allies against Protestantism.
- Treaty of Nonsuch in 1585 meant that Spain and England were at war in the Netherlands. The Armada was part of that war.
- England would be a useful addition to Spain's empire.

Provocation*

- Drake's actions in the New World angered Philip II.
- Elizabeth I's support for Dutch rebels angered Philip II.

Circumstances

- Spain acquired Portugal in 1580, increasing Spain's power and wealth.
- Spain's success in the Netherlands since 1579 gave them confidence.
- Elizabeth's hesitation to fight in the Netherlands showed weakness.

Figure 2.7 Why did Philip II launch the Armada against England in 1588?

Philip's strategy

With 130 ships, 2,431 guns and around 30,000 men, Philip II's Armada was the largest fleet Europe had ever seen. It was ordered to sail along the English Channel to the Netherlands to join up with the Duke of Parma. The Armada would transport 27,000 troops to Kent and march on London, get rid of Elizabeth and set up a Catholic government.

Key term

Provocation*

Making someone angry.

How did England defeat the Spanish Armada?

English ship design

One reason for English victory was its **ships**. Another was **long term planning**. England had been building new ships, called galleons. They had advantages over the Spanish ships (see page 87 for more information about galleons).

Although the English galleons were some of the best warships in the world, by 1588 England had only 24 new ships. So it was not just the better galleons that led to Spain's defeat.

English ships were smaller and could change direction quicker than Spanish ones.

English ships were faster than Spanish ones.

English guns took up less space, so there was enough room to fire and reload cannon quickly. The English were able to fire more cannonballs than the Spanish.

Figure: Why English ships were better than Spanish ones.

Spanish supplies

Spain's Armada had many problems.

- Food supplies – Drake's raid on Cadiz had destroyed supplies, so the Spanish were forced to make new storage barrels from poor quality wood. By the time they reached the Channel, a lot of their food was rotting.

- Cannonballs – the Spanish ships didn't have enough cannonballs and the ones they had were poor quality.

Key term

Fireships*

Empty ships set on fire and sent in the direction of the enemy to cause damage and confusion.

Planning and communications

Philip II's plan required Medina-Sidonia, commander of the Spanish fleet, to join with the Duke of Parma in the Netherlands. This was not a good plan for two reasons.

1 The Duke of Parma did not control any deep-sea ports where the large Spanish ships could dock. Instead everything had to be transferred from land to the ships using smaller boats, which took time.

2 Communications between Medina-Sidonia and the Duke of Parma went by sea and it took a week for a message to reach Parma that Medina-Sidonia was near to the Netherlands. It meant that Parma wasn't ready. It would take 48 hours to load troops onto the ships, and the English were ready to attack.

Figure 2.8 shows what happened during the Armada. In the end, England defeated the Armada.

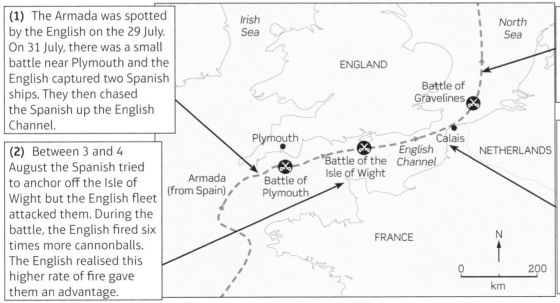

(1) The Armada was spotted by the English on the 29 July. On 31 July, there was a small battle near Plymouth and the English captured two Spanish ships. They then chased the Spanish up the English Channel.

(2) Between 3 and 4 August the Spanish tried to anchor off the Isle of Wight but the English fleet attacked them. During the battle, the English fired six times more cannonballs. The English realised this higher rate of fire gave them an advantage.

(4) The Spanish ships that remained had to sail around the north of Scotland. Bad weather meant many were shipwrecked and thousands of sailors died.

(3) The Armada had to ancho Calais while the Duke of Parm his troops ready to board. On night of 6 August the English fireships* into the Armada to chaos. On 8 August the Spanis and English fought a large ba called the Battle of Gravelines The faster, more mobile Englis ships with their faster-firing g defeated the larger Spanish s

Irish Sea
North Sea
ENGLAND
Battle of Gravelines
Plymouth
Battle of the Isle of Wight
Calais
English Channel
NETHERLANDS
Armada (from Spain)
Battle of Plymouth
FRANCE
N
0 200
km

Figure 2.8 The course of the Armada.

Should Philip II take the blame for defeat?

Although Philip II met with his commanders before the Armada sailed, he ignored their suggestions. Elizabeth, however, let her commanders (Drake, the Earl of Nottingham and Lord Seymour) take the decisions. Interpretation 1 is clear about Philip II's role in the defeat of the Armada.

Interpretation 1

One interpretation discussing why Philip II failed to invade England in 1588 from 'Why The Armada Failed' in *History Today Magazine* (1988).

Here, then, lay Philip's true error: he was not only an armchair strategist, but an armchair tactician too [he had no experience of war at sea] … the final version [of his plans] depended for success upon a tactical edge [superiority] which Spain's ships simply did not possess. In this disharmony [mismatch] between strategy and tactics, therefore, lies the true explanation of the Armada's fate.

What were the consequences of the English victory over the Spanish Armada?

While England was under threat of invasion, Elizabeth I addressed her troops at Tilbury, Essex. Source A is an extract from this famous speech.

Source A

Excerpt from Elizabeth I's speech to her troops at Tilbury, August 1588.

Let tyrants fear … I am come amongst you, … being resolved [determined], in the midst and heat of the battle, to live and die amongst you all; to lay down for my God, and for my kingdom, and my people, my honour and my blood, even in the dust.

I know I have the body but of a weak and feeble woman; but I have the heart and stomach of a king, and of a king of England too, and think foul scorn [think it ridiculous] that Parma or Spain, or any prince of Europe, should dare to invade the borders of my realm.

Defeating the Spanish was very good news for Elizabeth and boosted her image. A new portrait was commissioned (see Source B), she was the centre of a great parade through London and a special commemorative medal was made. It said 'God blew, and they were scattered'. This was an important point – God seemed to have favoured Elizabeth and Protestantism over Philip and Catholicism.

Source B

The Armada portrait of Elizabeth I, painted in 1588 by George Gower.

The Armada affected the countries involved in different ways.

1 **England:**
   - Defeating a stronger nation boosted English pride.
   - Showed the strength of the English navy and encouraged more ambitious trade and exploration.

2 **Spain:**
   - Spain's power declined after the Armada.
   - It cost a lot of money.
   - Philip II continued to fight Protestantism.

3 **The Netherlands:**
   - The defeat of Spain encouraged the Dutch rebels to carry on fighting Spain.
   - The alliance between England and the Dutch was strengthened.

Figure 2.9 Reasons for the defeat of the Armada in 1588.

Summary

- The Armada was the Spanish fleet sent to invade England in 1588.
- The English fleet set out from Plymouth and followed the Armada up the English Channel.
- The Armada had problems with supplies and communications.
- The English had faster ships that could fire more cannonballs from a greater distance.
- The Battle of Gravelines did substantial damage to the Armada.
- After Gravelines, the Armada headed north and thousands lost their lives in shipwrecks.
- The defeat of the Armada was a great boost for Elizabeth I, England and Protestantism in Europe.

Checkpoint

Strengthen

S1 Describe the key features of Philip II's plan to invade England.

S2 Give two advantages English ships had over Spanish ships.

S3 Give one example of how the Armada benefitted Elizabeth I.

Challenge

C1 Explain the importance of each of the following in the defeat of the Armada.
   - Philip II
   - English cannon.

If you are not confident about any of these questions, form a group with other students, discuss the answers and then record your conclusions. Your teacher can give you some hints.

Recap: Challenges to Elizabeth at home and abroad, 1569–88

Recall quiz

1 What and when were the four key plots against Elizabeth I?

2 Give two reasons why the northern earls revolted in 1569.

3 Give one reason why the 1570 papal bull of excommunication was so significant.

4 When were Catholic priests first smuggled into England?

5 Give two things stated by the Act for the Preservation of the Queen's Safety, 1585.

6 Why was the New World so important to Spain?

7 Between which years did Sir Francis Drake circumnavigate the globe?

8 Give two examples when Elizabeth I indirectly supported the Dutch Rebellion.

9 When was the Battle of Gravelines?

10 Give two reasons why the Spanish Armada failed.

Activities

1 Work in pairs to make a bar chart showing how the level of threat faced by Elizabeth I changed from 1569 to 1588. Choose up to six threats and give each a score out of ten according to how serious it was. A score of 10 would mean that England was invaded or Elizabeth I was overthrown, so a major threat. A score of 0 would mean no threat to Elizabeth I, at home or abroad.

2 Compare the events of 1569 and 1586. Would Elizabeth I have felt more under threat at the end of 1569 or 1586? Write a paragraph explaining your answer.

3 Why was Elizabeth I able to survive the challenges she faced 1580–1588? Write one paragraph on how she survived domestic challenges, and one on foreign challenges.

Activity

Make a timeline of the key events of the Armada from 31 July to 8 August 1588.

Activities

1 Work in groups of four. Study Figure 2.8 on page 61. Each take one factor explaining why Philip II launched the Armada in 1588. Explain and provide evidence for your factor.

2 Can you find any links between the different factors? Write down the links.

Writing historically: building sentences

Successful historical writing uses a range of sentence structures to help you be as clear and precise as possible.

Learning outcomes

By the end of this lesson, you will understand how to:

- link ideas with clarity and precision
- change sentence structure to emphasise key ideas.

Definitions

Clause: a group of words that contains a verb and can form part or all of a sentence.

Single clause sentence: a sentence containing just one clause.

Subordinating conjunction: a word used to link a dependent clause to the main clause of a sentence.

Compare the two drafts of sentences below, written in response to this exam-style question:

> Explain why Philip II launched the Armada against England in 1588.
>
> (**12 marks**)

These points are written in pairs of unlinked, **single clause sentences**.

The connection between these points is made clear with subordinating conjunctions.

Philip was angry with Elizabeth. She had offered support to Dutch Protestants who were rebelling against Spain.	Philip was angry with Elizabeth because she had offered support to Dutch Protestants who were rebelling against Spain.
Mary, Queen of Scots was executed in 1587. The Armada was already being prepared when news of the execution reached Philip.	Although Mary, Queen of Scots was executed in 1587, the Armada was already being prepared when news of the execution reached Philip.
Elizabeth was excommunicated by the pope in 1570. Philip openly supported all plots against Elizabeth's life.	After Elizabeth was excommunicated by the pope in 1570, Philip openly supported all plots against Elizabeth's life.

1. Which responses are more clearly expressed? Write a sentence or two explaining your answer.

Subordinating conjunctions can link ideas to indicate:

- an explanation: (e.g. 'because', 'as', 'in order that')
- a condition: (e.g. 'if', 'unless')
- a comparison: (e.g. 'although', 'whereas')
- a sequence: (e.g. 'when', 'as', 'before', 'until' etc.)

2. Find as many different ways as you can to use subordinating conjunctions to link these pairs of ideas.

- Mary, Queen of Scots, caused Elizabeth I a lot of trouble. Mary came to England as the Catholic alternative to Elizabeth's Protestant rule.

- Mary was involved in many plots against Elizabeth. She had the support of Philip II and the pope.

How can I structure my sentences for clarity and emphasis?

In sentences where ideas are linked with subordinate conjunctions, there is:

- a main clause that gives the most important point of the sentence

- a follow-on, subordinate clause that adds more information about that central point.

Different sentence structures can alter the focus of your writing. Look at these sentences that have been used to introduce responses to the exam-style question on the previous page.

Compare these two versions of the first sentence:

> Although Mary, Queen of Scots was executed in 1587, the Armada was already being prepared when news of the execution reached Philip. The Armada sailed in 1588.

This is the main clause in this sentence

This is a subordinate clause. It is linked to the main clause with a subordinating conjunction.

> The Armada was already being prepared when news of the execution reached Philip, although Mary, Queen of Scots was executed in 1587. The Armada sailed in 1588.

3. Which version do you prefer? Write a sentence or two explaining your decision.

In both responses, the second sentence is much shorter than the first sentence.

4. Experiment with different ways of organising the three pieces of information in the student's response above, linking all, some, or none of them with subordinating conjunctions:

- Mary, Queen of Scots, was executed in 1587
- the Armada was already being prepared
- the Armada sailed in 1588.

5. Which version do you prefer? One of yours, or the original version? Write a sentence explaining your decision.

Improving an answer

6. Now look at the notes below written in response to the exam-style question on the previous page.

> Philip was a staunch Catholic.
> Elizabeth had offered support to Dutch Protestants.
> Elizabeth was excommunicated by the pope in 1570.
>
> Throckmorton and Babington plots, supported by Philip and the pope.
> The Armada sailed in 1588.

a. Experiment with different ways of arranging and structuring all the information in sentences. Try to write at least two different versions.

b. Which version do you prefer? Write a sentence explaining your decision.

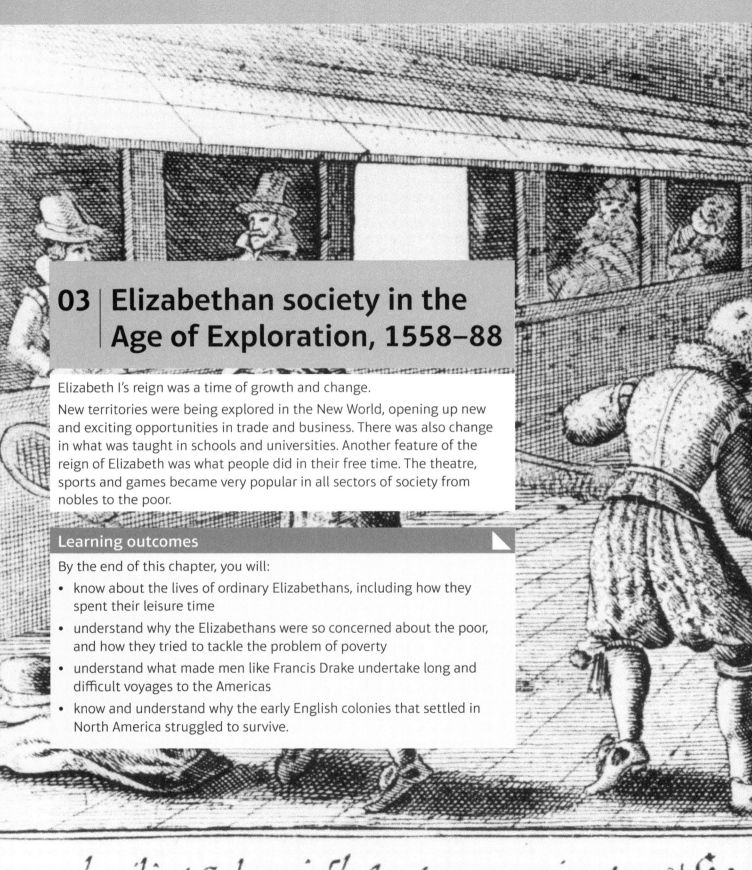

03 | Elizabethan society in the Age of Exploration, 1558–88

Elizabeth I's reign was a time of growth and change.

New territories were being explored in the New World, opening up new and exciting opportunities in trade and business. There was also change in what was taught in schools and universities. Another feature of the reign of Elizabeth was what people did in their free time. The theatre, sports and games became very popular in all sectors of society from nobles to the poor.

Learning outcomes

By the end of this chapter, you will:

- know about the lives of ordinary Elizabethans, including how they spent their leisure time
- understand why the Elizabethans were so concerned about the poor, and how they tried to tackle the problem of poverty
- understand what made men like Francis Drake undertake long and difficult voyages to the Americas
- know and understand why the early English colonies that settled in North America struggled to survive.

Quando pilà et Sphæræ flectuntur corporis artus.

Corpus erit levius, pectus erit levius.

3.1 Education and leisure

Learning objectives

- Understand Elizabethan attitudes to education.
- Know the different leisure activities pursued by Elizabethan society.

Education

Attitudes to education

There was no national school system in Elizabethan England. If you were given any education, then it prepared you for the life you were expected to lead. Education was not designed to increase social mobility*. Most people learned what they needed from their parents; these would be practical skills to earn money or run a household. Very few children went to school, and if they did, they would be boys rather than girls. School was not compulsory*.

New influences on education

Attitudes to education were beginning to change in Elizabethan England about education.

- Humanists* believed education was important for everyone and everyone should have the chance to fulfil their potential with a wide-ranging education.
- Protestants believed it was important to read and write so people could read the Bible.
- An increase in trade and business meant that it was important that more people could read and write.

Education in the home and at school

In spite of these new influences, any actual change in education was extremely limited. The figure below shows the type of education Elizabethan children might receive. Your education depended upon what your parents decided and could afford.

Key terms

Social mobility*
Being able to change your position in society.

Compulsory*
Something everyone has to do.

Humanist*
Someone who accepts scientific explanations rather than supernatural ones, who has no religious beliefs but makes decisions based on what is best for humans.

Apprenticeship*
Someone learning a trade or a skill. In Elizabethan times, apprentices were not paid – in fact, it cost money to be an apprentice.

Place in society	Boys	Girls
Nobility	Private tutors at home Latin, Greek, foreign languages, history, classics, philosophy, religion, government Horse riding, archery	
	Fencing, swimming, wrestling	Music, dancing, needlework
Wealthy middle classes, e.g. merchants, professionals, gentry	Petty school (see page 71) ↓ Grammar school ↓ University	• Usually taught by mothers. • Learned skills such as managing the household, preserving food, treating minor illnesses and injuries, baking, sewing, brewing. • Might be taught to read and write. • If so, taught either at home or at a Dame School (see page 71).
Other middle classes, e.g. business owners, skilled craftsmen	• Petty school and then a grammar school if they could afford it. • Apprenticeships*	
Tenant farmers, farm workers, unskilled labourers	• Possibly a Dame School, maybe a Petty school but no further. • Often no formal education. • Learned what was necessary from their parents.	• Possibly a Dame School. • Usually no formal education. • Learned what was necessary from their parents.

Figure: The education received by Elizabethan girls and boys.

Source A

A 16th-century woodcut showing a teacher and his pupils.

Grammar schools

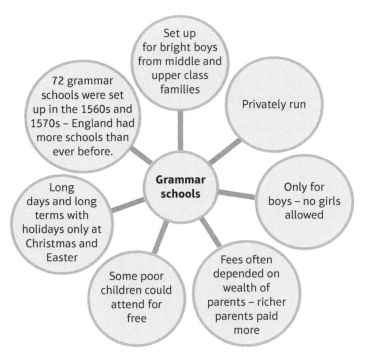

Figure: Grammar schools in Elizabethan England.

The focus of the curriculum was learning Latin, and also Ancient Greek and Roman history and philosophy. Boys spent a lot of time memorising texts, especially the Bible. Public speaking and debating were practised, as these were thought important for Elizabethan gentlemen. There was also time set aside for archery, chess, wrestling and running.

Below is a typical grammar school timetable, based on a real timetable from an Elizabethan grammar school in Wales.

	Monday–Thursday	Friday
6.00	Church – prayers	Church – prayers
7.00	Recite previous day's lessons by heart	Translate what was read the day before
7.30	Breakfast	Breakfast
8.00	Translation: Latin into English	Recite what has been learned so far this week
9.00	Study of works of Ancient Greek and Roman scholars – history, philosophy, literature, poetry	Recite what has been learned so far this week
11.00	Dinner	Dinner
12.00	Teacher questions class on what was read before dinner; homework marked while boys studied Latin or Greek grammar	Recite what has been learned so far this week
1.00	Translation to / from English, Latin, Greek or rehearse and act out Ancient Greek and Roman plays	Recite what has been learned so far this week
3.30	Afternoon break	Recite what has been learned so far this week
4.00	Grammar – or recite what has been learned so far this week	Teacher reads ancient texts to the class
5.00	School ends	School ends

Discipline and punishments

Children had to be well behaved inside and outside school. If they weren't there was a system of punishment, which included corporal punishment*.

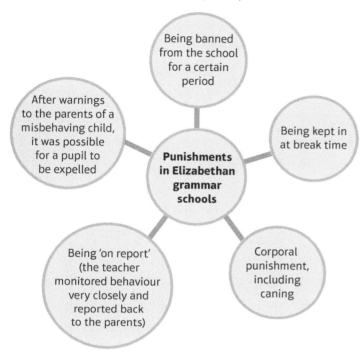

Figure 3.1 Punishments in Elizabethan grammar schools.

Merchants and craftsmen

Some grammar schools ran a slightly different curriculum for the sons of merchants and craftsmen. This focused on more practical subjects, such as English, writing, arithmetic and geography.

Skilled craftsmen and yeomen

There were grammar school places available for the sons of craftsmen and yeoman* farmers, too. However, most got their education through apprenticeships, or through their parents teaching them about the family business or farm.

Key terms

Corporal punishment*

Punishment where a person is hurt, often using something like a stick or cane.

Yeomen*

Farmers owning their own land.

Brew*

To make beer

Debating*

Two people with different views on a subject put forward their ideas and thoughts.

Petty schools

Boys attended petty schools before going to grammar school. Petty schools were often run in a teacher's home. Parents had to pay fees to send their children. Beating for bad behaviour or not doing well was common.

Schools for girls

Most girls did not go to school, but if they did they went to a Dame school.

They were called 'Dame' schools because they were often run by a local, educated woman and provided a basic education.

Women were not expected to support themselves, but would go from being under their father's care to their husband's. For most girls, education was focused on the home. As wives and mothers, they would need skills to cook, bake, brew*, sew and treat simple illnesses and injuries.

School	Who?	What?
Grammar schools	Boys aged 8–14	Latin, Greek, French. history and philosophy by writers from Ancient Greece and Ancient Rome. Public speaking and debating*. Learning long sections of the Bible and other texts. Archery, chess, wrestling, running.
Petty schools	Boys aged 4–8	English – reading and writing. Basic arithmetic
Dame schools	Girls aged 4–8	English – reading and writing. Basic arithmetic

Figure: The different schools in Elizabethan England.

Labourers and poor children

Most Elizabethans, whether girls or boys, had no formal, school-based education, as the majority of the population were farmers or labourers. They learned what they needed from their families, working on the land or in the home. In most cases, children needed to earn money from an early age to help the family out and there was no time or money for them to go to school.

How big an impact did schools have on Elizabethans?

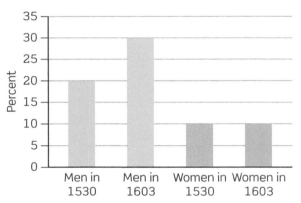

Figure: Percentage of people who could read and write in Elizabethan England.

The bar chart shows that the number of men who were literate* increased but the number of women stayed the same. A lot of wealthy Elizabethans talked about the value of educating women, but this had little impact on the number of girls being educated. The role of women continued to be as wives and mothers, whereas boys could use their education to earn a living.

Education in universities

There were two universities in Elizabethan England: Oxford and Cambridge. Very few people went to university. The boys who did go would usually start at the age of 14 or 15. They studied a variety of subjects including music, astronomy, medicine, Law and religion.

Oxford and Cambridge universities are made up of different colleges, many of which were started by the Tudors. Elizabeth wanted colleges to educate more Protestant clergymen to increase the number of well-educated, Protestant clergymen.

An alternative to university was to study to become a lawyer at the Inns of Court in London.

Key term
Literate*
Being able to read and write.

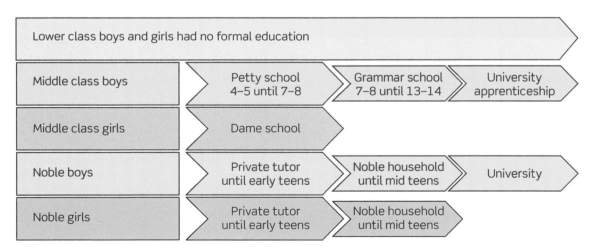

Figure 3.2 A summary of the different routes through education of Elizabethan children according to gender and class.

Activities ?

1   Write a paragraph describing what schooling you had for each of the following Elizabethan children:

   • a nobleman's son
   • a wealthy merchant's daughter
   • a craftsman's son.

2   Write a short paragraph explaining why and how education developed in Elizabethan times. You will need to talk about the growth of grammar schools and the new ideas about education.

3   Why would Elizabeth I be so keen to educate more Protestant clergymen at university during her reign? To help, think about what other events / issues she was dealing with in 1571 and 1584.

Leisure

Like all other areas of life in Elizabethan England, your leisure activities depended on your gender and place in society. And like all other areas, there were generally more opportunities for wealthy people and for men.

Participation in leisure – sport
Nobility and gentry

Sports played by the nobility included:

• hunting on horseback, with hounds (both men and women)
• hawking (men and women)
• fishing (men and women)
• fencing (men)
• real tennis (men).

Source B

Real tennis, from a 16th-century engraving. Real tennis was an indoor game played by upper class men. It was a cross between modern tennis and squash. Balls could bounce off the walls as long as they did not do go above a certain limit, otherwise it was out.

Quando pila et Sphæræ flectuntur corporis artus.
Corpus erit levius, pectus erit levius.

So oft ich thue den Ballen schlagn ,
Erfrisch ich mir hertz tragen vnd magn

Some sports were played by men of all social classes, although not together. Noble men wrestled in private. Men of a lower social class had public wrestling matches, but all classes would watch together. Gambling on the outcome was very popular.

Working people: craftsmen, farmers and labourers

Football was a game for lower class men. It was extremely violent and men were sometimes killed. Matches could last for hours. There were no rules against picking up the ball and running with it, or tripping up other players!

There were also no rules about the size of the pitches, the shapes of the goals or the number of players. Pitches included streets or the countryside between villages.

Spectator sports

Elizabethans loved watching sport. This included watching animals fight. Money was often gambled on the outcome.

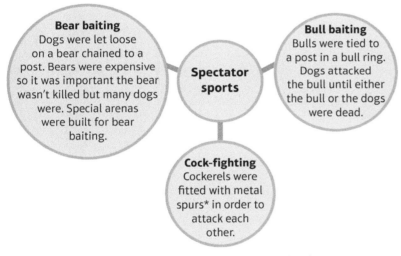

Figure: Spectator sports in Elizabethan England.

Baiting and cock-fighting were popular with all classes and even with Elizabeth I. However, Puritans* especially disapproved of them because the fights were usually held on Sundays, which they considered a holy day.

Key terms

Spurs*
A spike attached to the leg.

Puritans*
Extreme Protestants who strictly followed what the Bible said.

Below is a summary of who participated in which Elizabethan activities.

Activity	Upper classes	Lower classes
Hunting	Men and women	—
Fencing	Men only	—
Tennis (real)	Men only	—
Wrestling	Men only; in private	Men only; in public
Football	—	Men only
Baiting	Everyone together	
Cock-fighting		
Literature	Men and women	If literate
Theatre	Everyone together	
Playing music	Men and women	Men and women Only men could be paid musicians
Dancing	Men and women	Men and women

Figure: Elizabethan activities.

Pastimes

Literature

There was a lot of new literature written during Elizabeth I's reign. Popular subjects included history, tales of voyages of discovery and translations of Latin and Greek books. Creative writing, especially poetry, was very popular among well-educated people. Elizabeth herself wrote poetry.

Theatre

Theatre developed as a result of Protestantism. At the start of Elizabeth's reign, **mystery plays** were the most common form of theatre. These plays brought the Bible and saints' stories to life, but Protestants thought they promoted the Catholic Church. Elizabeth was concerned that they would encourage religious violence, so her government put a stop to them.

There was a sudden demand for new, non-religious plays. They were more exciting than the older religious plays, as unlike Bible stories, no-one knew the endings. Comedies were very popular because the Elizabethans had a rude sense of humour. Many theatre companies were formed, often by the nobility. The Earl of Leicester had his own company called **Leicester's Men**, and in 1583, Elizabeth I established **The Queen's Men**.

The popularity of plays led to the first purpose-built theatres. The first of these was the **Red Lion** in Whitechapel, London, constructed in 1567. There was also the Rose and the Globe in London (see Source C). Sometimes as many as 2,000 people could queue to see a performance.

Source C

A play being staged in Shakespeare's Globe theatre.

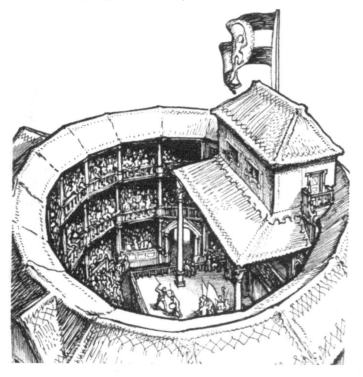

Music and dancing

Elizabethans of all classes loved music and many people played instruments.

	Wealthy families	**Poorer families**
Instruments they played	Lutes (like a guitar) Harpsichords (like a piano)	Bagpipes Fiddles (violins)
Where people listened to music	While eating or at feasts Church services Theatres	Fairs and markets Church services Taverns (pubs) Barber shops Theatres

Figure: Music in Elizabethan times.

New music was being written:

- to go with new plays that were being shown at the theatre
- for the new musical instruments that were becoming more popular.

Dancing was very popular and, although upper and lower class people did not dance together, it did bring men and women together.

The galleries. Richer people sat here as seats were expensive.

The Gallery above the stage had the most expensive seats. The view was not good but the rest of the audience could see you sitting in the expensive seats.

The pit. It only cost a penny to stand and watch the play here. This is where poor people would go.

The stage was where the actors performed. There were no women actors – female parts were played by boys.

Figure: An Elizabethan theatre.

Interpretation 1

Historian Andrew Wilson interprets Elizabethan England as one which changed dramatically, in the book *The Elizabethans* (2011).

There were new schools… English ships – sailed to new lands, and brought back… the sense of an expanded world. In churches, halls, palaces and country houses, new music delighted the ear. You could not be alive in Elizabethan England and not feel that it was a young country, full of [the ability] to reinvent itself.

Activity

Work in groups of four. Two people should look for evidence that supports the idea of Elizabethan leisure pursuits as being positive, exciting and improving; two should look at evidence against this view. When you have finished, deliver a short presentation to show to the rest of the class what conclusions you have come to.

Summary

- Education expanded during Elizabeth I's reign, but this expansion was limited. Of those who did get an education, most were boys. Most people were still illiterate.
- There was not a great difference in the academic education of noble girls and boys. However, noble boys were expected to be much more active outside of the classroom.
- Every town in England had a grammar school by 1577.
- Elizabethan pastimes were similar to modern ones, but sport was much more violent.
- Theatre thrived: there were many new plays and purpose-built theatres, and plays were popular with all classes in Elizabethan England.
- Protestantism led to the development of new plays.

Checkpoint

Strengthen

S1 Give two examples of Elizabethan schools and say who they were for.

S2 Give two examples of pastimes enjoyed by all Elizabethans.

Challenge

C1 Explain why literacy increased for males but not for females under Elizabeth's reign. Is this surprising, considering that England was under the rule of a young queen?

3.2 The problem of the poor

Learning objectives

- Understand the reasons why poverty and vagabondage increased in Elizabethan England.
- Understand how and why attitudes towards the poor shifted during Elizabeth's reign.

The main question to ask when reading the next section is: why was there an increase in poverty and vagabondage* between 1558 and 1588?

Who were the poor?

For ordinary Elizabethans, not being able to work meant a life of poverty. Unemployment and illness could lead to starvation. Different people in different places would find themselves in poverty at different times in their lives.

Elizabethan society was worried about those who:

- needed financial help (poor relief*) or charity (alms)
- begged or were homeless
- were 'itinerants' – people who had moved from their home parishes* looking for work. Modern historians sometimes identify the 'poor' as those who spent 80% of what they earned on buying bread.

Survey of the poor in Norwich (1570)

Of those found who needed, or would soon need, poor relief:

40% were under 16 years old
66% were women
25% of those women were over 60 years old.

- Families with an adult man in work often used 80% of their wage to buy food to avoid starvation.
- Households run by women were often poor because women were paid less than men.

Figure: Results of a survey carried out by the mayor of Norwich in 1570.

Key term

Vagabondage*

When people had no job or home and wandered about the countryside.

Why did poverty increase?

Population growth

During the reign of Elizabeth I, England's population grew by about 35%. It grew especially fast in towns and cities. London grew fastest of all. By 1603 it had a population of 150,000, ten times the size of England's second city, Norwich, which had a population of 15,000.

The growing population of towns and cities needed food but they didn't grow any themselves. Food was grown in the countryside and brought into towns and cities for sale. More people to feed meant the price of food in towns went up.

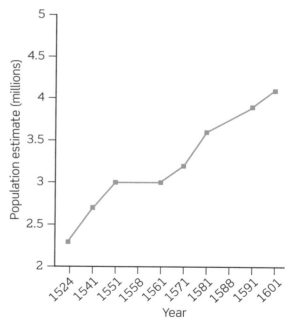

Figure 3.3 Population growth in Elizabethan England.

Key terms

Poor relief*

Financial help for the very poor paid for by a special tax that was raised and distributed by the local community.

Parish*

An area served by one parish priest.

Rising prices

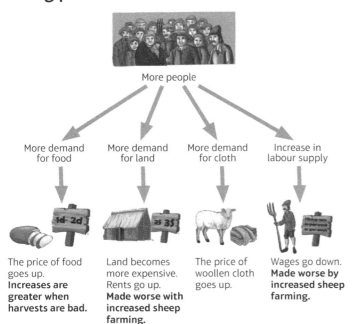

Figure: The growing population led to price rises and low wages. This contributed to increasing poverty.

Changes in the countryside: sheep farming

English wool was important to the Elizabethan economy.* It employed a lot of people. It made up 81.6% of England's exports*. Demand for woollen cloth was increasing, making the price rise. This meant lots of large landowners started sheep farming to make money. Sheep farming was blamed for increasing poverty in the countryside for many reasons.

- Land once used for crops or **common land*** was being used, taking away sources of food for people
- It did not take as much labour as growing crops, leading to unemployment.
- Some land was used to grow crops to feed to sheep during the winter, instead of crops to feed people.

Changes in the countryside: enclosure

Enclosing land meant:

- dividing up large fields farmed by whole villages into smaller fields owned by one person
- small farms being joined up to make bigger farms run by one farmer – the small farmers were evicted.

This meant that tenant farmers* lost their farms and farm labourers and villagers lost jobs and land to farm.

Key terms

Economy*

How a country makes money - it includes making, selling and buying things.

Exports*

Goods that are sold abroad.

Common land*

An area which everyone could use, for example, for grazing animals and collecting wood.

Tenant farmers*

Farmers who paid rent to a landowner to farm the land.

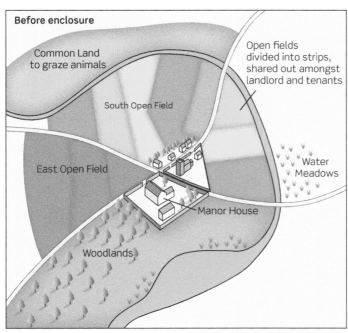

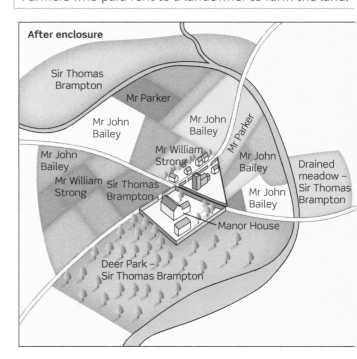

Figure 3.4 The impact of enclosure on a village.

Why did farmers enclose the land?

Enclosing the land allowed farmers to make improvements to how both crops and animals were farmed.

Before enclosure	After enclosure
Many people worked the land and there was no coordinated and effective way of growing crops or looking after animals.	Farmers wanted to do more arable farming* to take advantage of high food prices. Enclosing land made it easier to drain and fertilise* the soil so more crops could be grown.
Land was left **fallow** (unused) for a year for the soil to recover, which was a waste of land.	Crops were grown one year, and animals raised the next. The animals fertilised the land. Animals needed to be fenced in for this to work. The animals fertilised the land.
Animals **grazed** (ate grass) everywhere and anywhere. Livestock bred at random.	Animals were kept in one field. This allowed the farmer to produce better animals by only allowing the best to breed. It also prevented animals from trampling crops.

Figure: Farming before and after enclosure.

Why did enclosure cause poverty to increase?

Enclosure did not make landowners poor – they often grew rich. However, poor farmers and farm labourers became poorer.

Enclosure meant:

- the new farming methods needed fewer workers, so many people lost their jobs
- common land was enclosed, so villagers lost land where they could graze their animals and collect firewood. Without this land, poor subsistence farmers* were unable to survive.

Enclosure made people very angry (see Interpretation 1).

Key terms

Arable farming*

Growing crops on farm land.

Fertilise*

To add something to land that adds goodness to the soil, such as animal poo.

Subsistence farmers*

Farmers growing just enough to feed the family but not to sell.

Interpretation 1

In Ian Mortimor's *The Time Traveller's Guide to Elizabethan England* (2013), changes to the countryside are described as being a great cause of trouble.

… the destruction of arable fields and villages is a profound [serious] worry to the families who are evicted. It is equally worrying to the authorities in those towns where the homeless husbandmen [famers, land workers] go begging. The gradual loss of land to the working man and his family may fairly be described as the second-greatest single cause of unrest during the reign, second only to religion.

Land values and rents

As the money that could be earned from farming increased, landowners put up the rents of tenant farmers. Those who could not pay were forced off the land to make way for wealthier, more successful tenant farmers. Sometimes the land they left behind was enclosed instead.

How big was the problem of enclosure?

A pamphlet by Sir Thomas Smith, written in the 1560s, blamed gentry and yeomen for preferring to farm sheep to growing crops because they could get a good price for wool. A lot of people felt that growing food for people should be more important.

In fact, only 2–3% of land in England was enclosed by the end of the 16th century. Where it took place, however, it had a great impact and was blamed for the increase in the number of unemployed and vagabonds (see below).

Reasons for the increase in vagabondage

Vagabondage greatly worried Elizabethans, especially the government and nobility. Elizabethan society had a strict hierarchy in which everyone had a place. Vagabonds lived outside of this hierarchy as they had no place – no employer, no master, nowhere they belonged. Vagabonds were feared because often they sometimes had to commit crimes to survive and this threatened law and order.

The urban poor

Poverty and unemployment in the countryside caused people to move to towns to find work. The number of urban poor grew very fast in Elizabeth times. Until then it was thought that people who were able to work (but didn't) were simply lazy. Elizabeth I's government eventually realised that unemployment was a real problem, but they continued to treat vagabonds badly.

Key term

Economic recession*

When a fall in demand leads to falling prices and businesses losing money. This can lead to businesses failing and unemployment going up.

Activity ?

Create a flow chart to show how an increase in population led to rising prices, which in turn led to enclosure, then unemployment and vagabondage.

Figure: Reasons people were forced into vagabondage.

Changing attitudes and policies towards the poor

Impotent and able-bodied poor

Financial help for the poor came from:

- **poor relief** which was paid for by a local tax called the **poor rate**. It was collected and given out by Justices of the Peace (JPs*)
- charity from individuals.

Poor people were seen as either:

- **deserving** (impotent): unable to work because of age or illness
- **idle** (able-bodied): capable of working, but didn't.

Elizabethans were understanding to the deserving poor. The idle poor were treated harshly.

When trade was bad, especially the cloth trade, the number of abled-bodied poor increased. This was especially noticeable in towns because:

- there were so many of them
- people who lost their livelihoods in rural areas came to towns in search of work.

The cloth trade was especially bad in 1563–64, 1568–73 and 1586–88, so unemployment was a regular problem. This led to laws to help the poor. The key laws were passed in 1563, 1572 and 1576. How do these relate to the wool trade?

Key term

JPs*

Justices of the Peace – people given the job of keeping order in a community (see page 10).

Source A

A vagrant is tied and whipped through the streets as punishment. This engraving is from 16th-century England.

Government action

Poverty had always been dealt with locally. Elizabeth's government passed new, national laws. The main reason was fear of vagabonds and social unrest.

The 1572 Vagabonds Act was a turning point because:

- it established the first national poor rate
- it recognised unemployment as a real problem for the first time.

Rather than punishing the unemployed, the new law said towns must provide them with work.

1563 Statute of Artificers	1572 Vagabonds Act	1576 Poor Relief Act
Aim: to ensure that money to pay for poor relief was collected from people who owned land. Features: - anyone who refused to pay the poor rates could be imprisoned - officials failing to organise poor relief could be fined up to £20.	Aim: to deter vagrancy. Features: - vagrants to be whipped and a hole drilled through each ear - vagrants were imprisoned if arrested a second time and given the death penalty for the third. Also: - it established the national poor rate for the first time and helped the impotent poor - JPs were to keep a register of the poor - towns and cities had to find work for the able-bodied poor.	Aim: to help the able-bodied poor find work. Features: - JPs provided the able-bodied poor with raw materials* to make things to sell - those who refused work were sent to a special prison known as the house of correction.

The impact of the Elizabethan poor laws

Although there were changes for the better, poverty continued to be a major problem in Elizabeth I's reign. This was because of the conflict with Spain and the revolt in the Netherlands, which hit trade badly. Different towns and cities coped in different ways with the problem.

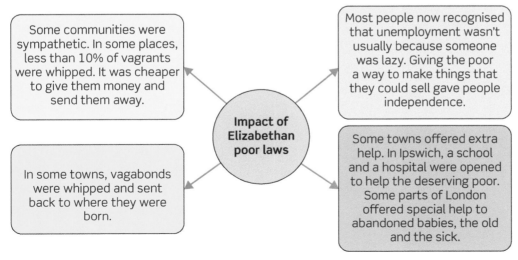

Figure: The impact of the Elizabethan poor laws from worst case to best.

Exam-style question, section B

Describe **two** features of the Elizabethan system of poor relief that were new.

4 marks

Exam tip

The word 'new' is very important. You won't be awarded marks for writing about things that stayed the same in Elizabethan times.

Summary

- Poverty and vagabondage were seen as growing problems in Elizabethan England.
- The Elizabethans generally divided the poor into categories: the 'idle' and 'deserving'.
- Population growth was one of the main reasons for the increase in poverty.
- Enclosure, disruptions to trade and rising prices also led to the increase in poverty.
- Attitudes to the poor changed as unemployment became recognised as a real issue.
- Elizabeth I's government passed parliamentary laws to tackle poverty and vagabondage.
- One change was that local officials were to provide raw materials, such as wool, for the unemployed so that they could make things to sell.
- Vagabonds faced harsh punishments, although few local authorities actually applied them.
- There were local attempts to help the poor as well, especially in towns like Ipswich.

Checkpoint

Strengthen

S1 Give two reasons why poverty increased in Elizabethan times.

S2 Explain why vagabondage increased in Elizabethan times.

S3 Describe one positive change in how Elizabethans treated the poor.

S4 Identify one Elizabethan Poor Law and say what it did to help the poor.

Challenge

C1 Can you identify one key turning point in the treatment of the poor and explain why it was so important?

Make sure you understand the definitions of important terms used in this section, such as 'vagabondage' and 'poverty', before answering these questions.

3.3 Exploration and voyages of discovery

Learning objectives

- Understand why Elizabethans wanted to explore the world.
- Know about Francis Drake and the significance of his circumnavigation of the globe.

What led Elizabethans to explore?

Expanding trade

The New World opened up new opportunities for Elizabethans. English merchants needed to look for new trading routes, as the conflict with Spain and in the Netherlands had hit the wool and cloth trade. Reports from the Americas suggested that there were many different crops, animal skins and precious metals to be found there.

Private investors*, including Elizabeth I, paid for many of the voyages of discovery. Although it was risky, it was also possible to make lots of money. Spain was becoming very rich mining for silver in Peru, as well as exporting crops such as sugar and tobacco. There were still vast areas of the Americas that had not been explored yet.

The Triangular Trade*

Slavery had existed for thousands of years across all continents, societies and cultures. During Elizabeth I's reign, English merchants began to transport African slaves to the New World. This slave trade caused misery to the slaves and made huge fortunes for the traders.

John Hawkins was a navigator, slave trader and the man behind some of the key improvements in the English navy that helped the Armada to be defeated (see page 61). He first bought slaves from Africa in 1562, transported them across the Atlantic and sold them to the Spanish colonists. He bought ginger, animal hides, sugar and pearls with the money he got for the slaves. He made a big profit and repeated the journey in 1564. This was the start of the **Triangular Trade**.

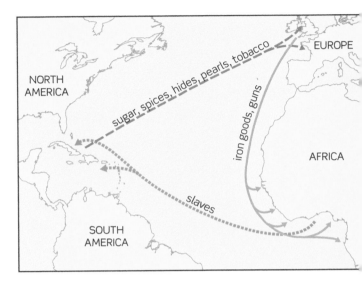

Figure 3.5 The early Triangular Trade that began to develop after John Hawkins' 1561–62 voyage.

Adventure

Some young Elizabethan men, especially from the gentry and nobility, went on voyages of discovery and exploration in the hope of adventure and making their fortunes.

Key terms

Investors*

People who provide money to fund a project or business in the hope that they will get their money back plus more.

Triangular Trade*

Trade from Europe to Africa to America and back to Europe. European goods were sold, African slaves bought and taken to the Americas. They were exchanged for sugar, spices and other exotic goods.

New technology

Navigation

Navigation was becoming more precise. New methods of navigation were published in books. For example, by 1584, the English mathematician Thomas Harriot worked out a simpler way of accurately calculating the direction a ship was heading in. This made voyages safer, more direct and faster.

Since the 15th century, quadrants* and astrolabes* had been used to work out a ship's position using the stars. Accurate navigation was important for long voyages of discovery. Explorers started recording their voyages and publishing them, allowing others to follow their routes.

Source A

An illustration from a 1551 French sailing manual showing how to use an astrolabe.

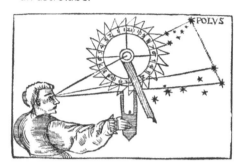

Key terms

Quadrant*

Similar to an astrolabe, it was used by sailors to help with navigation at sea. It was the shape of a quarter circle.

Astrolabe*

An instrument used by sailors to help with navigation at sea. It was circular.

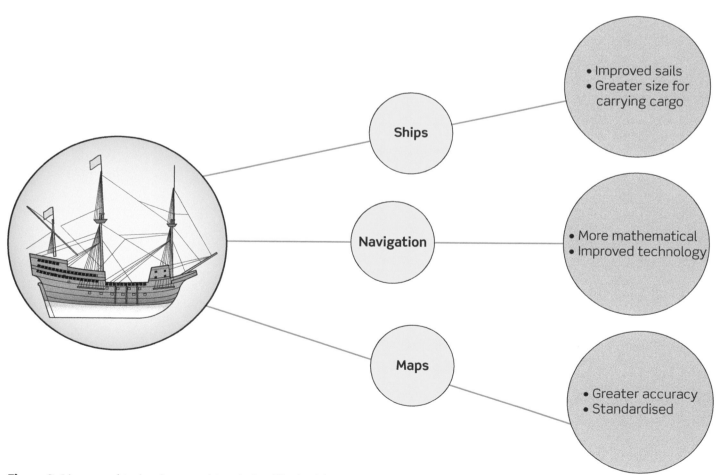

Ships
- Improved sails
- Greater size for carrying cargo

Navigation
- More mathematical
- Improved technology

Maps
- Greater accuracy
- Standardised

Figure 3.6 Improved technology on ships during Elizabeth's reign.

Key terms

Longitude*

How far east or west you are.

Latitude*

How far north or south you are.

Maps

Improved navigation led to more accurate maps. In 1569, the Mercator map was developed. It used lines of longitude* and latitude* to give sailors a much more accurate picture of the world. Being able to print maps meant that sailors could all have the same map rather than hand drawn ones that could all look different.

Source B

A world map made by Gerardus Mercator, printed in 1587. The world's geography is clearly recognisable.

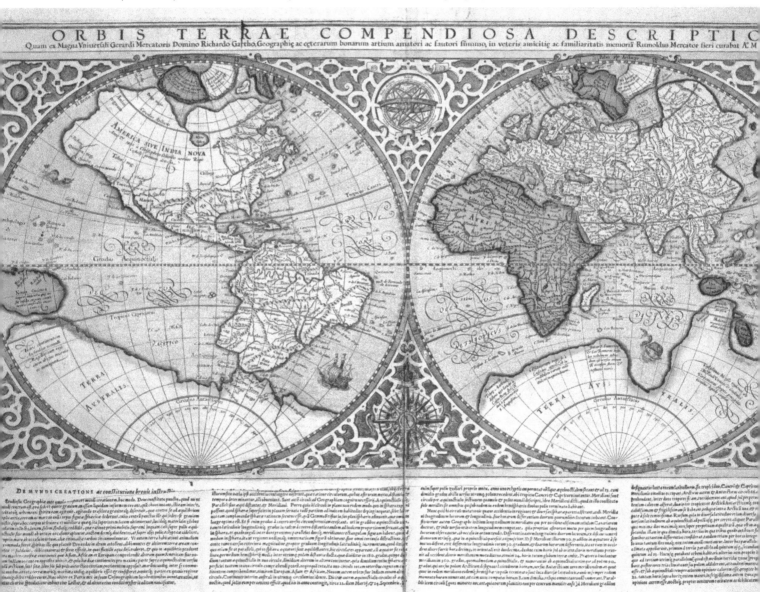

Ship design

Extend your knowledge

Shipyards

Because there were many new shipyards built during the Elizabethan period, better ships could be built in larger quantities.

Larger, more stable ships

Ship design improved, making longer journeys possible. Traditional ships were replaced by larger, better, **galleons**.

How galleons were different	Impact
They were larger	More supplies could be carried for longer journeys. More cargo could be transported.
They had lower forecastles and aftcastles	These were higher sections at either end of the ship. They used to be very tall, but the new galleons had smaller 'castles' making the ships more stable and safer in rough seas.
They had more masts	More masts meant more sails, which meant faster voyages.
They had different sail types	Earlier English ships only had square sails. Galleons used a mixture of square sails for speed and triangular 'lateen' sails that made them easier to steer.
They had gun decks running the length of the ship	Cannons could fire from the sides of the ship as well as from the bow and stern. This made it easier for galleons to defend themselves against attacks from pirates or Spanish ships.

Figure: How galleons were different and better.

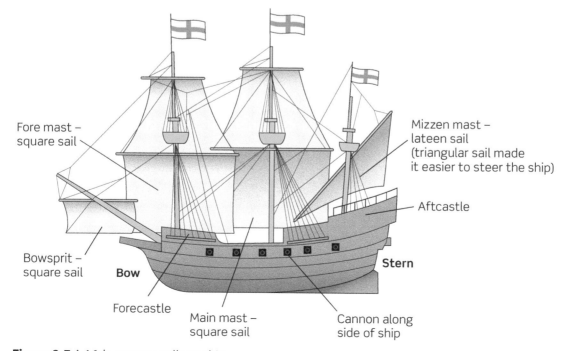

Figure 3.7 A 16th-century galleon ship.

Key terms

Circumnavigation*

To travel all the way round the world.

Colonies*

Lands under the control or influence of another country, occupied by settlers from that country.

Drake's circumnavigation of the globe

Drake's circumnavigation* of the globe took almost three years, from December 1577 until September 1580. Following this achievement, he was knighted by Elizabeth I.

Why did Drake circumnavigate the globe?

Drake had not set out with the aim of being the first Englishman to sail around the world. His main purpose was to raid Spanish colonies* in the Pacific. Relations with Spain were becoming worse and Elizabeth wanted to harm Spanish trade and colonies.

Interpretation 1 supports the idea that circumnavigation was an accident.

Interpretation 1

C.E. Hamshere plays down the significance of Drake's circumnavigation of the globe as a happy accident, in the book *Drake's Voyage Around the World* (1967).

What is fairly evident [clear] is that Drake did not set out to perform the feat [act] of circumnavigation. He probably carried the possibility in the back of his mind, but his prime object was to plunder [attack and rob] the Spaniards, not to make a voyage of exploration. The discoveries he did make were incidental [were by accident].

Although Drake and Elizabeth had political reasons for the voyage, they also expected to make huge profits. Drake returned from the voyage with treasure valued at up to £500,000,000 in today's money. This made Drake and his investors very wealthy.

What was the significance of Drake's circumnavigation?

England as a great sea-faring nation

Drake's voyage almost ended in disaster but in the end was an amazing achievement because:

- Drake set out with five ships, but by the time he had reached the Pacific ir 1578, he had only one left: the *Golden Hind*
- Drake and his 56 crew were only the second crew in history to circumnavigate the world
- it was a great boost to English morale
- it made English ships and sailors seem like the finest in the world
- it made the English more confident that they could deal with threats from Spain.

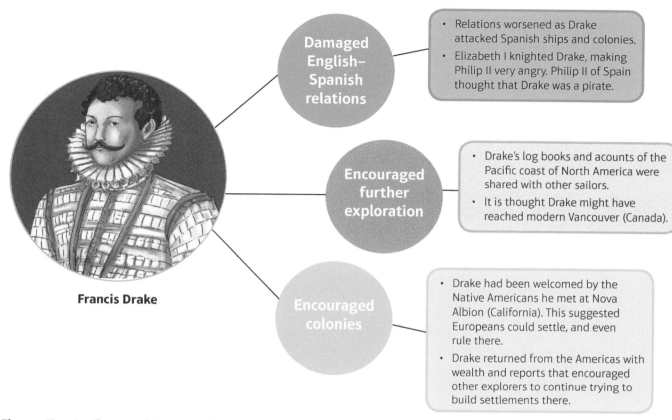

Francis Drake

Damaged English–Spanish relations
- Relations worsened as Drake attacked Spanish ships and colonies.
- Elizabeth I knighted Drake, making Philip II very angry. Philip II of Spain thought that Drake was a pirate.

Encouraged further exploration
- Drake's log books and acounts of the Pacific coast of North America were shared with other sailors.
- It is thought Drake might have reached modern Vancouver (Canada).

Encouraged colonies
- Drake had been welcomed by the Native Americans he met at Nova Albion (California). This suggested Europeans could settle, and even rule there.
- Drake returned from the Americas with wealth and reports that encouraged other explorers to continue trying to build settlements there.

Figure: The significance of Francis Drake's circumnavigation of the globe 1577–80.

Extend your knowledge

Davy Ingram

One of the most famous accounts of the Americas was written by Davy Ingram. After being stranded in Mexico, he walked 3,000 miles north up the Atlantic coast of America. He told fantastic tales of great wealth to be found, including precious metals, minerals, fertile soil and bright red sheep and rabbits. These tales encouraged more voyages of exploration.

Nova Albion

Elizabeth I and other European rulers did not recognise the agreement made by the pope almost a century earlier that gave the Americas to the Spanish and Portuguese. Elizabeth gave her explorers the right to take any land that no other Christian leader had claimed. The rights of the Native Americans to the land were not considered. In June 1579, Drake was forced to land north of what is now San Francisco to repair his ship. Here he was welcomed by Native Americans. Drake decided to name the region Nova Albion and declared that Elizabeth I was its queen.

Activity ?

List as many reasons as you can why voyages of exploration were so dangerous.

Activities ?

1   List all the positives and negatives that you can find that happened during and after Drake's circumnavigation of the globe.

2   Explain why Philip II was angry that Elizabeth I knighted Drake.

3   Imagine that you are a sailor having returned from Drake's circumnavigation of the globe. Write two or three diary entries about what has happened and why this journey was so important. You should say why the journey has been so hard, what the high points of the voyage were and what happened at Nova Albion.

Summary

• Trade was the driving force behind voyages of exploration.

• Undermining Spain's position in the New World was another important reason for voyages of exploration, especially as English–Spanish relations were getting worse.

• New technology made ships better at undertaking longer journeys.

• New technology also led to more accurate maps and navigation.

• Printing enabled the reproduction of standardised maps, navigation manuals and accounts of the fabulous riches to be found in the New World, encouraging more exploration.

• Drake's circumnavigation of the globe began as a mission to attack Spanish colonies.

• Nova Albion encouraged the English to attempt the further colonisation of North America.

• Drake's circumnavigation was extremely profitable and encouraged more investment in voyages of exploration.

Checkpoint

Strengthen

S1 Give two reasons why there were voyages of exploration during Elizabeth I's reign.

S2 How did improved technology help encourage long voyages?

S3 Give one reason why Drake circumnavigated the globe 1577–80.

S4 Give one consequence of Drake's circumnavigation of the globe.

Challenge

C1 Which technological development do you consider the most important in encouraging voyages of exploration and why?

If you are not confident about any of these questions, form a group with other students, discuss the answers and then record your conclusion. Your teacher can give you some hints.

3.4 Raleigh and Virginia

Learning objectives

- Understand the significance of the attempts to colonise Virginia.
- Understand why the attempts to colonise Virginia failed.

Timeline
The colonisation of Virginia

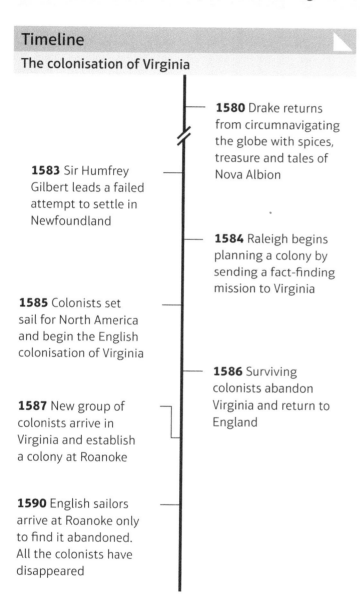

1580 Drake returns from circumnavigating the globe with spices, treasure and tales of Nova Albion

1583 Sir Humfrey Gilbert leads a failed attempt to settle in Newfoundland

1584 Raleigh begins planning a colony by sending a fact-finding mission to Virginia

1585 Colonists set sail for North America and begin the English colonisation of Virginia

1586 Surviving colonists abandon Virginia and return to England

1587 New group of colonists arrive in Virginia and establish a colony at Roanoke

1590 English sailors arrive at Roanoke only to find it abandoned. All the colonists have disappeared

Walter Raleigh's significance

Walter Raleigh was born into a wealthy, gentry family and was a courtier during the reign of Elizabeth I. He was also a writer, historian, and explorer.

In 1584, Walter Raleigh was given money from Elizabeth I to explore and settle in lands in North America. Previous failed attempts to build settlements meant it was hard for Raleigh to persuade people to go on the expeditions. Also, Raleigh was not planning on going on the expeditions himself because Elizabeth did not want to lose one of her favourite courtiers. However, Raleigh did contribute by:

- organising and raising money
- persuading people to go on the voyage
- appointing a governor to rule in Virginia.

Investigating and promoting the Virginia project

Raleigh sent a fact-finding expedition to Virginia in North America in 1584. The expedition reported back that the Native Americans were friendly and that this part of North America was a paradise.

Raleigh used these findings to persuade a group of English men to leave their homes and make the dangerous voyage across the Atlantic. They were convinced that they would find their fortunes in Virginia. This was important because in London, other travellers had spread rumours of fantastical monsters and brutal savages in America.

Raising funds

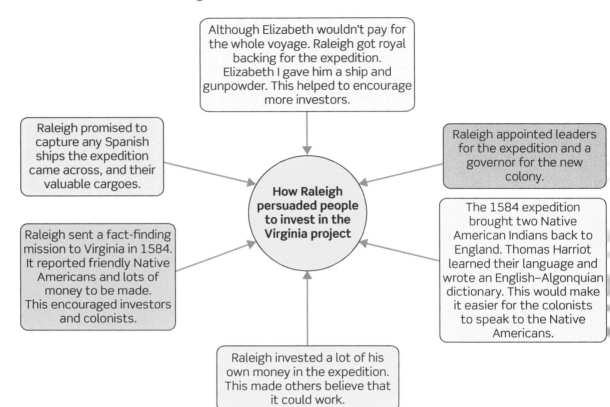

Although Elizabeth wouldn't pay for the whole voyage. Raleigh got royal backing for the expedition. Elizabeth I gave him a ship and gunpowder. This helped to encourage more investors.

Raleigh promised to capture any Spanish ships the expedition came across, and their valuable cargoes.

Raleigh appointed leaders for the expedition and a governor for the new colony.

How Raleigh persuaded people to invest in the Virginia project

Raleigh sent a fact-finding mission to Virginia in 1584. It reported friendly Native Americans and lots of money to be made. This encouraged investors and colonists.

The 1584 expedition brought two Native American Indians back to England. Thomas Harriot learned their language and wrote an English–Algonquian dictionary. This would make it easier for the colonists to speak to the Native Americans.

Raleigh invested a lot of his own money in the expedition. This made others believe that it could work.

Figure: How Raleigh persuaded people to invest in the Virginia project.

Extend your knowledge

The Algonquian people

The native people in the region that the English wanted to settle were mainly Algonquian. The English fact-finding expedition in 1584 met a local chief, Wingina, who ruled several small settlements on Roanoke Island. The Algonquian people had their own political system, culture and laws. The English colonists who expected to be able to take over and govern the land and its people, found that they had to work with the local people rather than rule them.

As well as the money that would come from investors it was thought money could also be found by:

- bartering* with the Native Americans
- providing work for English cloth makers and merchants who would supply the colony
- gold and tobacco produced by the colony being sent back to England to be sold.

By 1585, Raleigh had raised the money needed to fund the expedition.

Key term

Bartering*

Exchanging goods for other goods, instead of paying money for them.

Who?

About 300 colonists with a variety of skills:
- landowners
- craftsmen (e.g. blacksmiths, carpenters, stone-masons, weavers)
- hunters (and hunting dogs) and fishermen
- clergy
- soldiers to protect the other colonists
- farmers to grow food and look after animals to feed the others

Supplies?

Enough:
- food to feed everyone on the voyage across the Atlantic and up until the first harvest
- fresh water for the voyage
- tools and raw materials for the craftsmen
- farming tools
- seeds for planting
- weapons
- salt for preserving food

When to sail?

- In enough time for a crop to be planted on arrival in the colony (a good harvest was essential to see the colonists through the winter)
- When they have enough colonists of the right kind

Ships?

- Big enough to carry colonists and supplies
- Armed with cannon, in case of attack by Spanish or pirates

Other problems to think about

Will need to:
- protect the colony from possible Spanish attack
- buy animals in the Caribbean first for eating and breeding
- build shelters and a fort as soon as they arrive
- have a good supply of seeds of different sorts
- barter with the Native American Indians for things the colonists need
- find a leader as Elizabeth won't allow Raleigh to go on the voyage
- raise enough money

Figure 3.8 Raleigh's organisations and planning to prepare for the voyage to Virginia.

Organising the Virginia project

Finding colonists and sailors

Finding people willing to give up their life in England to go to Virginia as colonists and sailors willing to cross the Atlantic was difficult. In the end there were 107 men, rather than the 300 Raleigh had hoped for. There were no women. Almost half were soldiers, but there were landowners, farmers and skilled craftsmen.

However, Elizabeth wouldn't allow Raleigh to lead the expedition. She didn't want to lose one of her favourite courtiers. Instead, the following men were put in charge.

Who	Role	Suitability
Richard Grenville	Expedition commander	Grenville was a very experienced sailor and soldier, but he took risks. He did not get on with Ralph Lane, the governor of Virginia.
Ralph Lane	Governor of Virginia	Lane was an expert fort builder. He was also an explorer and a soldier with a 'can do' attitude.
Thomas Harriot	Translator and cartographer	Harriot could speak the native language, Algonquin. He understood navigation and was skilled at making maps.

Ships and timing

Raleigh sent five ships to Virginia: *Tiger*, *Roebuck*, *Lion*, *Dorothy* and *Elizabeth*. The *Tiger* was the largest and carried meats, vegetables, beer, wine, seeds and grain to make bread. The ships left England on 9 April 1585, but this would already be too late for the colonisers to plant crops that they would need to see them through the winter. The English landed on Roanoke Island in late 1585.

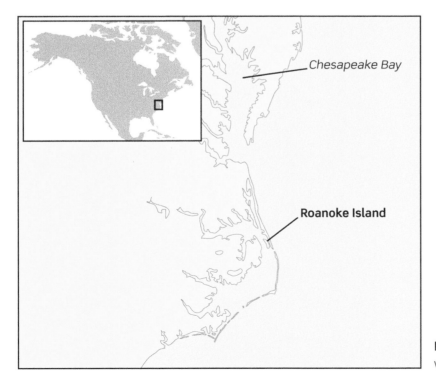

Chesapeake Bay

Roanoke Island

Figure 3.9 Roanoke Island and the surrounding area where the English colonists first settled.

Why was the colonisation of Virginia significant?

One reason that the Virginia colony was significant was that it **undermined Spain**.

- Virginia was a good position to attack Spain's New World colonies in Florida and the Caribbean.
- A British colony would give Native Americans an alternative to Spanish rule.
- A successful colony in Virginia would encourage more English colonies to be set up.

The second reason why the colony in Virginia was significant was because of **economic benefits**.

- As trade in Europe was difficult because of the conflict with Spain, it was hoped that Virginia would provide a new market for English goods.
- Valuable new crops could be grown in Virginia, especially tobacco and sugar.
- Mediterranean goods, like fruit and spices, that were difficult to obtain because of the conflict with Spain could be grown in Virginia.

Interpretation 1

Kupperman argues that privateering* was important as a reason for Elizabethan colonisation, in the book *Roanoke* (2007).

The desire to establish colonies in America was inseparable in these early years from privateering. When Raleigh decided to found the colony at Roanoke, his major reason was that it could serve as a base for privateering.

Key term

Privateering*

Merchants and explorers who captured foreign ships for their cargo.

Why did the attempts to colonise Virginia fail?

There were **two** attempts at colonising Virginia. Both failed. The first colony failed for a number of reasons.

The voyage

The colonists had left England too late to plant crops in Virginia. The food supplies and the seeds they brought were ruined when one of their ships, *Tiger*, ran aground and was damaged.

Arriving too late and without the right supplies, the colonists were unable to feed themselves. They made friends with the local Algonquian people, who gave them food – at first.

The colony was not what they hoped

Many colonists had hoped to get rich quick, but no precious metals were found. Some were not prepared to work hard and forage for food to help the colony survive.

Cooperation

The colonists did not work well together. Merchants and gentlemen did not want to do any physical work. Farmers did not want to work the land for the upper classes – they wanted their own land to farm. There were too many craftsmen and not enough farmers. The hunters quickly ran out of gunpowder so they could not hunt wild animals. The soldiers did not have the skills to farm land.

Figure: The first colony at Roanoke, Virginia, 1585-86.

Inexperience

The colonists became reliant on the Native Americans for survival. Raleigh had tried to think of everything, but he was inexperienced, and the right people were not sent on the voyage.

Interpretation 2

Giles Milton suggests, in his book *Big Chief Elizabeth* (2000), that the colonists themselves were the main reason for the colony's failure.

But unbeknown to either the Spanish or the English, Ralph Lane's settlers were proving more than capable of destroying themselves.

Native American resistance

The local chief, Wingina, who ruled Roanoke Island, at first welcomed the settlers. However, he soon became hostile to the settlers because:

- they constantly demanded food handouts
- Native Americans seemed to die mysteriously after the English visited them – the English brought new diseases that the Native Americans had not seen before
- there were some violent clashes between Native Americans and the settlers over food.

In spring 1586, Wingina asked other chiefs to help him attack the English. The governor, Ralph Lane, was prepared for the attack and Wingina was killed. However, Lane decided the colony was doomed. Lane and the colonists left Virginia and arrived back in Portsmouth in July 1586.

Exam-style question, Section B

'The main reason that voyages of exploration were undertaken during Elizabeth I's reign was to increase England's wealth.' How far do you agree?

You may use the following in your answer:

- English–Spanish relations
- developing trade.

You **must** also use information of your own.   **16 marks**

Exam tip

You can make a link between developing trade and English–Spanish relations, which were worsening. Remember, much of Spain's wealth was from its colonies in the New World.

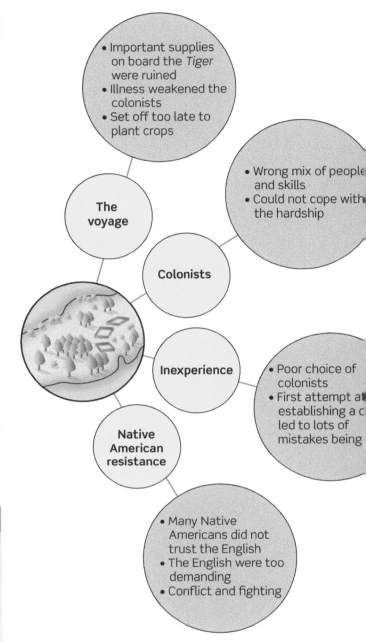

- Important supplies on board the *Tiger* were ruined
- Illness weakened the colonists
- Set off too late to plant crops

The voyage

- Wrong mix of people and skills
- Could not cope with the hardship

Colonists

- Poor choice of colonists
- First attempt at establishing a c led to lots of mistakes being

Inexperience

Native American resistance

- Many Native Americans did not trust the English
- The English were too demanding
- Conflict and fighting

Figure 3.10 Why did the Virginia Colony fail in 1585–86?

Source A

A painting of one of the Indian settlements. It is of Secotan in Virginia c1590. It was painted by John White, an artist sent to Virginia by Walter Raleigh.

Activity

How many examples of bad luck can you find to explain why the first colonisation of Roanoke 1585–86 didn't work?

Extend your knowledge

Thomas Harvey and Thomas Harriot

The colonists who returned to England in 1586 were angry. They said they had been promised great things but had been let down. They were especially cross with the colony's leaders. One person, Thomas Harvey, lost most of his money and was taken to court. He used his trial to tell people how cross he was.

Thomas Harriot wrote a book to give a different side to the story. It painted a glossy picture of what Virginia had to offer.

Roanoke 1587–90 (the second colonisation attempt)

A second attempt at colonising Virginia set out from England in 1587. This time there were 17 women and several families on board. Many colonists came from poor areas of London. Each was guaranteed 500 acres of land to farm. They were used to hardship and willing to work hard.

Raleigh put John White in overall charge. White had survived the first colony and knew what to expect. One of the Native American who had come to England in 1584 also went to encourage the local people to co-operate.

The Indians were hostile from the start. John White's adviser, George Howe, was found dead with 16 arrow wounds.

John White was asked to go back to England to update Raleigh on what had happened. When he returned to Roanoke, three years later in 1590, there was no-one there. What happened to the settlement remains a mystery. It is thought that hurricanes might have destroyed it, but this does not explain what happened to the colonists as no trace of them was ever found.

Extend your knowledge

Croatoan

The word 'Croatoan' was found carved on a post in the deserted colony. Some think this might mean that the colonists moved to live with the natives in the nearby Croatoan settlement.

THINKING HISTORICALLY — Cause and Consequence (3c&d)

Causation and intention

1   Work on your own or with a partner to identify as many causes for the failure of the Virginia colony in 1585–86 as you can. Write each cause on a separate card or piece of paper.

2   Divide your cards into those that are to do with:

    a   the actions of people

    b   the beliefs held by people at the time

    c   politics, society or economics

    d   long-term situations that have developed over time.

3   Look at the intentions (plans) and actions of the key people in the run-up to the failure of the Virginia colony in spring 1586: Sir Walter Raleigh, Ralph Lane, Chief Wingina, a gentleman colonist. For each person, write their name in the middle of a piece of paper and then write around the name:

    a   their intentions in 1585

    b   the actions they took to achieve these

    c   the consequences of their actions (both planned and unplanned)

    d   the extent to which their intentions were achieved.

4   Discuss the following questions with a partner:

    a   Did any one person plan for the Virginia colony to fail in spring 1586?

    b   How important are people's intentions in explaining the failure of the Virginia colony in spring 1586?

Summary

- Walter Raleigh was behind two attempts to establish an English colony in Virginia.
- England's colonies in Roanoke failed due to inexperience, the suitability of the colonists and the resistance of local American Indians.
- Conditions in Virginia were much harsher than the colonists were expecting.
- Many of the 1585 colonists did not co-operate with each other.
- The English were very dependent upon the local American Indians to survive.
- The local Indian chief, Wingina, did not trust the English and turned hostile.

Checkpoint

Strengthen

S1 Give two reasons why the English wanted a colony in Virginia.

S2 Give two reasons why Walter Raleigh was important in setting up the colonies.

S3 Give two reasons why the colonies failed.

Challenge

C1 Explain how the following led to the failures of the 1585 and 1587 colonies:

    a   bad luck   b   poor planning.

If you are not confident about any of these questions, form a group with other students, discuss the answers and then record your conclusion. Your teacher can give you some hints.

Recap: Elizabethan society in the Age of Exploration, 1558–88

Recall quiz

1 What were the two main types of school in Elizabethan times?

2 How did literacy rates change in Elizabethan England?

3 What two key developments were there in theatre during Elizabethan times?

4 Give three reasons for increasing poverty in Elizabethan England.

5 What three Acts of Parliament were passed to tackle poverty in Elizabethan England?

6 Give two important changes in the treatment of the poor in Elizabethan England.

7 Give three technological developments that improved Elizabethan sea voyages.

8 Give two causes and two consequences of Drake's circumnavigation of the globe.

9 Give three reasons why settling in Virginia was so important to the English.

10 Give three reasons why England's attempts to colonise Virginia failed.

Exam-style question, Section B

Explain why the attempt to colonise Virginia in 1585–86 was a failure.

You may use the following in your answer:

- the colonists
- Wingina.

You must also use information of your own.   **12 marks**

Exam tip

Organise your information before you answer. You have been given two prompts for reasons that you can write about. Try to think of one more reason to include before you begin writing.

Activities

1 Use the table to help remind you of the difference in the two voyages to Virginia during the late 1580s. Do you think any lessons were learned by the 1585–86 failure to colonise Virginia? List as many as you can think of.

When	1585–1586	1587–1590
Who	About 100 male settlers; a mix of landowners, craftsmen, soldiers and farmers	about 150 settlers, 17 women; many came from the London poor
Fate	Many could not cope with the hardship; relations with the Native Americans failed and Ralph Lane abandoned the colony; many died from hunger	117 left in Virginia in August 1587; English ships on a supply mission three years later found the colony abandoned; all the colonists had disappeared

2 To what extent was the failure of the 1585–86 attempt at colonisation Walter Raleigh's fault? Work in fours. One pair must prepare a case for the prosecution (against Raleigh), the other, a case for the defence (for Raleigh). Present this to the class, who will be the jury.

3 As you listen to the case for and against Raleigh, make a note of the evidence you think is the strongest. Once this is done, decide whether Raleigh was to blame or not. Write up your own, individual decison (verdict) in 150–200 words. Your verdict must include factual evidence.

Writing historically: writing cohesively

When you explain events and their consequences, you need to make your explanation as clear and concise as possible.

Learning outcomes

By the end of this lesson, you will understand how to:

- use pronouns to refer back to ideas earlier in your writing
- use sentence structures to help you refer back to ideas earlier in your writing clearly and economically.

Definition

Pronoun: a word that can stand in for, and refer back to, a noun, e.g. 'he', 'she', 'this', 'that', etc.

How can I refer back to earlier ideas as clearly as possible?

Look at the beginning of a response to this exam-style question below:

> 'The main reason that voyages of exploration were undertaken during Elizabeth I's reign was to increase England's wealth.' How far do you agree? **(16 marks)**

> *Before Elizabeth encouraged voyages of exploration, Spain controlled much of the New World and was very wealthy. This was a major factor in Elizabeth's desire to discover and claim new land outside of England.*

1. In the second sentence, the **pronoun** 'this' refers back to the first sentence. What could it refer back to?

a. Spain's wealth   **b.** Spain's control of the New World   **c.** Elizabeth encouraging voyages of exploration   **d.** it's not clear – it could be referring to any or all of them

One way in which you can improve the clarity of your writing is to avoid imprecise pronouns like 'this' and either:

- repeat the idea you are referring back to OR
- replace it with a word or phrase that summarises the idea.

2. Which of these would you choose to replace 'this' with to make these sentences as clear and precise as possible?

a. Spain's wealth   **b.** Spain   **c.** the New World   **d.** Elizabeth's ideas

3. Now look at another sentence from the same response. What could you replace 'This' with to make the sentence as clear as possible?

> *Sir Francis Drake impressed Elizabeth and the rest of the nobility of England when he circumnavigated the globe, brought back lots of treasure and made his investors very rich. This persuaded Elizabeth to knight him on the deck of the Golden Hind.*

How can I structure my sentences to make referring back even clearer?

4. Look at the three versions below of sentences written in response to the exam-style question on the previous page:

Version A

> *Before Elizabeth promised her support to Dutch Protestants, the Netherlands provided great trade links with England because they exported cloth and were under Spanish control. This was significant because it angered Philip of Spain, damaging relations.*

The pronoun 'this' is meant to refer back to this phrase – but, because it follows this clause, the writer has added doubt as to whether 'this' refers to the trade links between the Netherlands and England, the exports of cloth or the influence of Spain on the Netherlands.

Version B

> *The Netherlands provided great trade links with England because they exported cloth and were under Spanish control before Elizabeth pledged her support to Dutch Protestants. This was significant because it angered Philip of Spain, damaging relations.*

Version C

> *Before Elizabeth pledged her support to Dutch Protestants, the Netherlands provided great trade links with England because they exported cloth and were under Spanish control. This change in foreign policy was significant because it angered Philip of Spain, damaging relations.*

Which version is most clearly expressed and therefore easiest to read? Write a sentence or two explaining your ideas, thinking about: the use of the pronoun 'this', the position of the idea it refers back to and the use of a word or phrase that summarises the idea.

Did you notice?

When you read a text, you usually assume that the pronoun 'this' refers back to the piece of information that you have just read – not the one before that, or the one, two, or three sentences ago.

5. Why are these sentences below unclear and difficult to make sense of?

> *Philip began plans to invade England. After Elizabeth supported the Dutch Protestants and Drake's voyages in the Pacific, she knighted him on the deck of the Golden Hind. This greatly angered Philip.*

Improving an answer

6. Experiment with two or three different ways of rearranging and / or rewriting these sentence fragments below to create sentences that explain as clearly as possible why Philip wanted to invade England.

> *[1] Dutch Protestants rebelled [2] with Elizabeth's help [3] because she didn't want to lose her only Protestant allies in Europe. [4] This resulted in Philip planning the Armada.*

Preparing for your GCSE Paper 2 exam

Paper 2 overview

Paper 2 has two sections. Section B will have your questions on Early Elizabethan England. These are worth 20 per cent of your GCSE History assessment. The whole exam is 1 hour 45 minutes. You should use no more than 50 minutes to do Section A. That will leave time for Section B, which is your British Depth Study on Early Elizabethan England.

History Paper 2	Period Study and British Depth Study			Time 1 hour 45 mins
Section A	Period Study	Answer 3 questions	32 marks	50 mins
Section B	Tudor Depth Option B4	Answer 3 questions	32 marks	55 mins

British Depth Option B4 Early Elizabethan England, 1558–88

You will answer Question 5, which is in three parts:

(a) Describe two features of... (4 marks)

You are given a few lines to write about each feature. Allow five minutes to write your answer. It is only worth four marks, so keep the answer brief and do not try to add more information on extra lines.

(b) Explain why... (12 marks)

This question asks you to explain the reasons why something happened. Allow 20 minutes to write your answer. You are given two stimulus (information) points as prompts to help you. You do not have to use the prompts but they might be helpful to give you ideas. Higher marks are gained by explaining a point of your own in addition to the prompts. You will be given at least two pages in the answer booklet for your answer. This does not mean you should try to fill all the space. The front page of the exam paper tells you 'there may be more space than you need'. Aim to give at least three explained reasons.

(c) (i) OR (ii) How far do you agree? (16 marks)

This question is worth half your marks for the whole of the Depth Study. Make sure you have kept 30 minutes to answer it. You have a choice of statements: (i) or (ii). Before you decide, be clear what the statement is about: what 'concept' it is about and what topic information you will need to respond to it. You will have prompts to help, as for part (b).

The statement can be about: cause, significance, consequence, change, continuity, similarity or difference. Look at examples of questions to practise working out which of these things the statement is about. You could do this with everyday examples and test one another, for example:

- *the bus was late because it broke down* = statement about cause
- *the bus broke down as a result of poor maintenance* = statement about consequence
- *the bus service has improved recently* = statement about change.

You must make a judgement on **how far you agree.** Plan your answer before you begin to write, thinking about points for and against (see the diagram below). You should give at least three points. You **must** make sure your points all help answer the question.

Don't forget that you must write a conclusion, explaining how much you agree with the statement in the question. For example, you should say what you think was the most important cause, change or consequence and why.

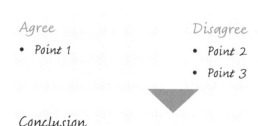

Agree
- Point 1

Disagree
- Point 2
- Point 3

Conclusion

Paper 2, Question 5a

Describe **two** features of Mary, Queen of Scots' threat to Elizabeth I. **(4 marks)**

Basic answer

Some people said that Mary, Queen of Scots, had a stronger claim to the English throne than Elizabeth I.

Some Catholics plotted to put Mary, Queen of Scots, on the throne.

The answer gives two features, but there is no supporting information.

Verdict

This is a basic answer because two correct features are given, but there is no supporting information.

Use the feedback to rewrite this answer, making as many improvements as you can.

Good answer

Some people said that Mary, Queen of Scots, had a stronger claim to the English throne than Elizabeth I. Some Catholics thought that Elizabeth was illegitimate and should not be queen of England.

There were Roman Catholic plots to put Mary, Queen of Scots, on the throne. The Ridolfi plot of 1571 was organised by an Italian Catholic banker with support from the pope.

The answer has identified two features, with extra information about each one. It describes what some Catholics thought of Elizabeth I's claim. It also gives an example of a plot with details about who was involved in it.

Verdict

This is a good answer because it gives two clear features of Mary, Queen of Scots' threat to Elizabeth I and gives extra detail to make the descriptions more precise.

Paper 2, Question 5b

Explain **why** Philip II launched the Armada against England in 1588.

You may use the following in your answer:

- England's involvement in the Netherlands
- Drake's attacks on Spain's colonies in America.

You **must** also use information of your own. **(12 marks)**

Exam tip

Don't tell the story of the events. Focus on explaining 'why'. Aim to give at least three reasons.

Basic answer

Philip II was the king of Spain. He was a Catholic who hated Protestantism. Philip had a big empire in America as well as the Netherlands, so Spain was very wealthy.

This information does not answer the question. It is background and does not explain why Philip II launched the Armada.

The Treaty of Nonsuch said England would help the Dutch rebels. Robert Dudley led an army to the Netherlands. This treaty made Philip want to attack England.

This says the Treaty of Nonsuch was a reason Philip II launched the Armada but does not give an explanation. It needs to say what happened because of the Treaty to anger Philip.

Drake had attacked Spain's colonies in America, making Drake lots of money. After he sailed round the world, Elizabeth I knighted Drake, making Philip II very angry because he saw Drake as a pirate. Drake singed the king of Spain's beard.

There is an explanation in this paragraph, which is good. The singeing of Philip II's beard is a good point but it has not been used to help explain why Drake's actions made Philip launch the Armada.

Philip II did not like Protestantism. He had sent a big army to the Netherlands to get rid of it there, and Elizabeth had helped anyone prepared to fight against the Spanish. Also, Philip was involved in lots of plots against Elizabeth. When the Armada was launched, England and Spain were at war. However, the Armada was defeated by the English and destroyed as the Spanish ships sailed home around Scotland.

There is a reason why Philip launched the Armada: Elizabeth's actions. It needs a couple of examples to show how it led to the Armada. The last sentence does not get any marks as it is not relevant to the question.

Verdict

This is a basic answer because:

- information is accurate, but it is weak because a lot of it is not relevant to the question
- it gives one or two reasons why the Armada was launched, but no developed explanations
- some of the answer is focused on the question, but it needs more details and examples.

Use the feedback to rewrite this answer, making as many improvements as you can.

Preparing for your exams

Paper 2, Question 5b

Explain **why** Philip II launched the Armada against England in 1588. **(12 marks)**

Good answer

In The Treaty of Nonsuch in 1585 Elizabeth promised to help the Dutch Protestants fight the Spanish. Elizabeth sent an army to the Netherlands but because they belonged to Spain it meant that England and Spain were at war. Philip II could not ignore it. So the Treaty of Nonsuch was important in explaining why Philip launched the Armada.

This paragraph gives a clear reason why Philip II launched the Armada with some accurate detail about the treaty.

Elizabeth I sent Drake to raid Spain in October 1585. He singed Philip's beard, which means he destroyed lots of Spanish ships and supplies in Cadiz harbour. This was a serious attack on Spain. Then Drake raided the New World. Elizabeth had ordered him to attack Spanish ships and lands there before, in 1577 for example. Philip II saw Drake as a pirate, yet Elizabeth I knighted him.

The information on Drake's 1585 attacks is good. It also shows it was not just his one attack in 1585 that angered Philip II. But this paragraph should go on to link the raids to Philip's decision to launch the Armada.

Philip II's religious beliefs were also important. He wanted to stamp out Protestantism, and Elizabeth I was a Protestant. The pope had called for her to be overthrown. This is what Philip intended to do with the Armada. So Philip II's religious beliefs are also important because that is why he wanted to overthrow Elizabeth.

A reason is given for the Armada that is not in the question. It also gets straight to the point, develops an explanation and reinforces the point at the end.

Verdict

This is a good answer because:

- it mainly focuses on the question
- there is no irrelevant background description or unnecessary information
- it supports the reasons with evidence to develop explanations.

The answer could be improved further by clearly linking each point back to why the Armada was launched.

Paper 2, Question 5c

Population growth was the main reason why vagabondage increased in Elizabethan England.
How far do you agree? Explain your answer.
You may use the following in your answer:
- sheep farming
- rising prices.

You must also use information of your own. **(16 marks)**

Exam tip

Consider points 'For' and 'Against' the statement and make a judgement. Be clear about your reasons for agreeing or disagreeing.

Basic answer

Vagabonds were homeless people. They wandered around looking for work, sometimes stealing or begging. Elizabethans saw vagabonds as a big problem. They believed everyone had a place in society, but vagabonds didn't belong anywhere.

As the population of England grew, so did the number of vagabonds because people got poorer. More people meant food prices rose. Rents went up, too, causing homelessness, so people became vagabonds. People in the countryside believed life in towns would be better so they left their villages. Some towns became overcrowded, like London, so people built shacks outside the city walls.

Sheep farming and new farming methods were becoming more popular. Drainage and fertiliser needed enclosed fields. People at the time thought that there was a lot of enclosure, but it is now known that only 2% of land was enclosed.

There were lots of different reasons why people were poor, like being too old, sick or disabled. Women were paid less than men, making them very poor if they didn't have a husband. This is why new laws about poverty and vagabondage were introduced.

Overall, there was an increase in vagabondage in Elizabethan England because the population grew so fast.

The introduction is all unnecessary background information. Nothing in this paragraph answers the question.

The second paragraph tries to explain a little about how population growth led to more vagabonds. It is not very developed and ends with a description that does not answer the question.

The third paragraph gives some accurate information about farming methods and enclosure, but it is not linked to vagabondage.

Although it is all accurate, paragraph 4 is not making a link between why people were poor and the increase in vagabonds. This means it is not answering the question.

The conclusion needs to explain *how far* population growth was to blame, rather than just saying it was to blame.

Verdict

This is a basic answer because:
- it shows some knowledge and understanding of the issue
- not all of the information used is linked to answering the question
- it gives some reasons for vagabondage, although these are not developed into explanations
- there is a conclusion about why the number of vagabonds increased, but it is too short and does not say **how far** it was caused by population growth.

Use the feedback to rewrite this answer, making as many improvements as you can.

Paper 2, Question 5c

Population growth was the main reason why vagabondage increased in Elizabethan England.

How far do you agree? Explain your answer. **(16 marks)**

Good answer

Vagabonds were poor people who did not have anywhere to live. They wandered the country hoping to find work, and sometimes begging and stealing. Their numbers increased as the population of England was growing fast, which led to rising prices. However, there were other changes, like new ways of farming and enclosure.

Population growth was probably the most important reason for the increase in vagabondage. More people meant rising demand for food, land and jobs, leading to rising prices and rents and falling wages. All these things combined to make more people poorer. Although some got poor relief, others became vagabonds.

Sheep farming also led to unemployment in the countryside. It was very profitable, so landowners turned land from crops to keeping sheep. Where this happened, unemployment rose as sheep did not need as many people to look after them. So people lost their jobs and some became vagabonds.

Woollen cloth was 80% of England's exports. When trade wasn't so good it could lead to unemployment. The conflict with Spain in the Netherlands between 1568 and 1573 led to a downturn in trade and increase in unemployment, making the government pass the Vagabonds Act in 1572.

Population growth was the most important reason why poverty and vagabondage increased in Elizabethan England. Downturns in trade was also an important reason, causing high unemployment.

The introduction shows that the student is focused on the question. It also suggests another reason why the number of vagabonds grew.

Straight away, in paragraph 2 the student looks at the reason given in the question and explains how population growth led to an increase in vagabonds. Another cause is clearly explained in paragraph 3. No information given is unnecessary and it is all linked to answering the question.

Paragraph 4 explains the student's own reason. This reason is not mentioned in the question. It explains how downturns in trade increased vagabondage and supports its point with accurate and specific information.

Although the conclusion is not long, it does answer the question of how far population growth was to blame for the increase in vagrancy. Remember, you do **not** have to agree with what is suggested in the question.

Verdict

This is a good answer because:

- it answers the question directly
- it gives a reason other than those mentioned in the question
- explanations have been developed and supported with accurate and precise evidence
- the conclusion answers how far population growth was to blame.

The answer could be improved further by expanding the conclusion so it explains *why* population growth was more important than trade.

Answers to Elizabeth Recap Questions

Chapter 1

1. Made up of 19 leading courtiers, advisers, nobles and government officials chosen by the monarch; met at least three times a week; presided over by monarch

2. The Act of Uniformity, the Act of Supremacy and the Royal Injunctions

3. Answers could include: fines; oath of supremacy; visitations; clergy who did not agree risked losing their positions; preaching licences; Ecclesiastical High Commission

4. The north and west of England

5. Answers could include: 400 clergy losing their positions; many areas in England were still Catholic, e.g. Lancashire; Vestment Controversy; Crucifix controversy

6. 1566

7. The Treaty of Edinburgh; to establish a Protestant government in Scotland

8. Her husband, Henry Stuart, Lord Darnley

9. Answers could include: Mary, Queen of Scots' claim to throne could be stronger; English Catholics might support Mary, Queen of Scots; 1569 plot against Elizabeth I involving Mary, Queen of Scots

10. The Duke of Norfolk

Chapter 2

1. Revolt of the Northern Earls 1569; Ridolfi plot 1571; Throckmorton plot 1583; Babington plot 1586

2. Answers could include: religion – earls were Catholic; loss of influence at court; desire to replace Elizabeth I with the Catholic Mary, Queen of Scots; Elizabeth I refused to name an heir or to marry

3. Answers could include: it encouraged Catholics to overthrow Elizabeth; it said Catholics no longer had to obey Elizabeth; it encouraged plots (e.g. the Ridolfi plot); it meant Elizabeth I could no longer be sure of her Catholic subjects' loyalty

4. 1574

5. In the event of Elizabeth I's assassination, Mary, Queen of Scots would be barred from succession; action could only be taken against Mary, Queen of Scots, or anyone else benefitting from Elizabeth's death, after a proper investigation and trial

6. It was a source of wealth (trade in tobacco, sugar cane, silver)

7. 1577 and 1580

8. Answers could include: funding the Dutch rebels; sending mercenaries to the Netherlands; raiding Spain's settlements in the New World, disrupting the flow of silver to Spain

9. 8 August 1588

10. Answers could include: Spain's provisions ran out; superior English ships and firepower; problems of communication between Medina-Sidonia and Parma; Parma was not ready or able to help engage the English; Battle of Gravelines; luck – bad weather around British coastline

Chapter 3

1. Petty and grammar

2. Literacy rates for men went up from 20% to 30%; there was no change for women

3. First purpose-built theatres; new, secular plays / banning of mystery plays

4. Answers could include: population growth; unemployment / economic recession; rising prices / wages not rising as fast; enclosure – although this last one is debatable

5. 1563 Statute of Artificers; 1572 Vagabonds Act; 1576 Poor Relief Act

6. Answers could include: unemployment was recognised as a genuine cause of poverty; national poor relief; helping able-bodied poor to find work / make things to sell

7. Answers could include: galleons could store more provisions; Harriot's improved method of navigation using the Sun; Mercator maps; more stable ships; more masts and sails

8. Answers could include: Causes – revenge on Spain, attacking Spanish colonies, profit; Consequences – Spain angered, Drake knighted, Nova Albion founded, England established as great sea-faring nation, huge personal wealth for Drake

9. Answers could include: base from which to attack Spanish colonies in the New World; development of English colonies for trade and wealth; New World could provide goods that previously came from Mediterranean, which was often dangerous for traders; prevent Spanish domination of New World

10. Answers could include: colonists arrived too late to plant crops; supplies being ruined; colonists; American Indians' hostility; colonists not co-operating with each other

Index

Key terms are capitalized initially, in bold type with an asterisk.
Headings for topic booklets are shown in italics.

Acknowledgements

4, 22 Hodder Education: Historians Turvey and Heard look at the effectiveness of Elizabeth's settlement in *Change and Protest 1536–88: Mid-Tudor Crises?* (1999); **14 Routledge:** Historian Christopher Haigh interprets Elizabeth as a strong, independent female leader in the book *Elizabeth I* (1988); **24 Hachette UK:** Written by an observer attending an open-air preaching event at Dedham, Essex, in 1575; **27 Hodder Education:** From The Reign of Elizabeth: England 1558–1603, Barbara Mervyn writes about the effectiveness of Elizabeth's religious policies (2001); **34 Penguin Random House:** Historian Susan Brigden discusses the threat of Mary, Queen of Scots, in her book, *New Worlds, Lost Worlds* (2000); **43 Cambridge University Press:** A letter to Philip II written by Guerau de Spes, Spain's ambassador to Elizabeth's court, on 8 January 1569; **46 Ignatius Press:** A raid on a Catholic house in Northamptonshire, described by a Catholic priest, John Gerard; **48 Francis Walsingham:** Sir Francis Walsingham in a letter to Lord Burghley (William Cecil) in 1575. He was writing about trying to stop the plots surrounding Mary, Queen of Scots; **52 Osprey Publishing:** Historian Angus Konstam talks about Francis Drake in *The Great Expedition* (2011); **53 History Today Ltd:** From an account of Elizabeth I's meeting with Francis Drake before he set sail in 1577; **57 Hodder Education:** An extract about Elizabeth's involvement in the Netherlands from *Elizabeth I: Meeting the Challenge, England 1541–1603* (2008) by John Warren; **63 History Today Ltd:** One interpretation discussing why Philip II failed to invade England in 1588 from 'Why The Armada Failed' in *History Today Magazine* (1988); **63 Elizabeth I of England:** Excerpt from Elizabeth I's speech to her troops at Tilbury, August 1588; **76 Penguin Random House LLC:** Historian Andrew Wilson interprets Elizabethan England as one which changed dramatically, in the book *The Elizabethans* (2011); **79 Penguin Random House LLC:** In Ian Mortimor's *The Time Traveller's Guide to Elizabethan England* (2013) changes to the countryside are described as being a great cause of trouble; **88 History Today Ltd:** C.E. Hamshere plays down the significance of Drake's circumnavigation of the globe as a happy accident in the book *Drake's Voyage Around the World* (1967); **95 Rowman & Littlefield Publisher:** Kupperman argues privateering was important as a reason for Elizabethan colonisation in the book *Roanoke* (2007); **96 Hodder and Stroughton:** Giles Milton suggests, in his book *Big Chief Elizabeth* (2000), that the colonists themselves were the main reason for the colony's failure.

Photographs

(Key: T-top; B-bottom; C-centre; L-left; R-right)

Cover: The Bridgeman Art Library Ltd/ English School, (16th century) / National Portrait Gallery, London, UK

The Bridgeman Art Library Ltd: English School, (16th century) / National Portrait Gallery, London, UK 15, Private Collection 6, 30, Peake, Robert (fl.1580–1626) (attr. to) / Private Collection 7tr, 8, Scottish school, (16th century) / Hardwick Hall, Derbyshire, UK / National Trust Photographic Library 7c, 33, English School, (16th century) / Burghley House Collection, Lincolnshire, UK 11, English School, (16th century) / Private Collection / The Stapleton Collection 26, Dutch School, (17th century) / National Galleries of Scotland, Edinburgh 40, 47, Hogenberg, Franz (1540–c.1590) (after) / Bibliotheque Nationale, Paris, France 55, Netherlandish School (16th century) / Koninklijk Museum voor Schone Kunsten, Antwerp, Belgium / © Lukas - Art in Flanders VZW 57tr, English School, (16th century) / Parham House, West Sussex, UK / Photo © Mark Fiennes 59 English School, (16th century) / Private Collection 63, English School, (16th century) / Private Collection 68, 73, Hodges, Cyril Walter (1909–2004) / Private Collection 75 **Alamy Stock Photo:** Pictorial Press Ltd 12, **TopFoto:** Bridgeman Images 18, Fotomas 81, World History Archive 85, Mercator, Gerardus (1512–94) / Private Collection 86, British Library Board 97 **Getty Images:** Heritage Images 57tc, **Mary Evans Picture Library:** 70